This publication has been made possible through the valuable
support of these partners of the Barefoot Guide Connection

GENERATIVE LEADERSHIP

Releasing Life in a Turbulent World

By The Sixth Barefoot Guide Writers' Collective

This Barefoot Guide 6 is
dedicated to the Fellows
of the Leading Causes of Life
Initiative and those they
work with in seeking to
support and enhance
greater life and a moral
vision in their communities
and societies.

THE BAREFOOT GUIDE 6
CONTRIBUTORS' COLLECTIVE

Writers

Laura Parajon Chancien, Nicaragua

Jim Cochrane, South Africa

Teresa Cutts, USA

Nomvula Dlamini, South Africa

Gary Gunderson, USA

Marcellino Jonas, South Africa

Mosi Kisare, Tanzania

Horst Kleinschmidt, South Africa

Sandy Lazarus, South Africa

Anita Marshall, South Africa

Kirsten Peachey, USA

Doug Reeler, South Africa

Liz Smith, South Africa

Craig Stewart, South Africa

Soma Stout, USA

Lisa Swanepoel, South Africa

Beulah Tertiens-Reeler, South Africa

Emily Viverette, USA

Other Contributors

Walter Flores, Guatemala

Jørn Lemvik, Norway

Aziz Royesh, Afghanistan

Editorial Team

Jim Cochrane

Teresa Cutts

Gary Gunderson

Doug Reeler

Craig Stewart

Beulah Tertiens-Reeler

Illustrator

Zach Stewart (zacharypstewart@gmail.com)

Colourization, done with permission by the editors, is not the responsibility of the illustrator

Cover Art

René Navarro (rene.a.navarro@gmail.com
   http://trauco-rene.deviantart.com
   https://atelier1741.wordpress.com
   https://www.instagram.com/
   rene.a.navarro/

Production

Layout artist – Paula Wood
   (paula@paulawooddesign.co.za)

Proof-reader – Beulah Tertiens-Reeler

The Writeshop Facilitators

Doug Reeler, CDRA & Barefoot Guide
   Connection, South Africa

Nomvula Dlamini, CDRA & Barefoot Guide
   Connection, South Africa

Liz Smith, independent practitioner,
   South Africa

Beulah Tertiens-Reeler, independent
   practitioner, South Africa

Administrators

Dawn Hall, Wake Forest - USA

Lisa Swanepoel, South Africa

Tasneem Wise, UCT - South Africa

Financial Support

Andy McCarroll

Doug Easterling

Jerry Winslow

Doug McGaughey

Heather Wood Ion

Emily Viverette

Organisational Support

LCLI Fellows

Community Development Resource
   Association – CDRA

CONTENTS

1   INTRODUCTION

What's this book about?

Giving Life a Chance
Our story is not your story
Reality Check
Who are we, why are we writing?

9   CHAPTER 1

RELEASING LIFE: Let the river flow

A river becomes a canal
Canalized Leadership
Encouraging a river back to life
Bringing leadership back to life
Releasing the Bird (poem)

19   CHAPTER 2

POISONING THE RIVER: Life under threat

Leadership for life in the face of death
On not being overcome
Releasing energy through lament
Integrating hurt & hope
"Failing forward" together

31   CHAPTER 3

THE RIVER'S JOURNEY: Re-authoring the World

Re-authoring the world
For what ends do we lead?
Social forms of leadership
Emerging forms of social change leadership & organization

53   CHAPTER 4

WORKING INSIDE THE RIVER:
Practicing Leadership within the Turbulence

Dragons can be beaten
Embracing the untamed life
Community Defenders
Boundary Leadership
Gustavo's story: AMOS Health & Hope
Four dimensions of wisdom for generative leadership
Generative insight: Observing the whole river

77 CHAPTER 5

LIVING IN THE RIVER: Aspects of a Leader's Being

Living in time and space, being present
Artistry in the lived moment: "Playing with infinity"
Holding the space & the person
Being a presence
Marcellino's story
Leading Love
The Reluctant Leader
The Intuitive Guide

97 CHAPTER 6

FLOWING FORWARD: Possibility above Actuality

"Possibility above actuality"
Out of South Africa: A personal tale
The nobility we are
Practices for change-makers
A different vision: "Fullness of life"
Radical inclusion
The Holy Longing (poem)

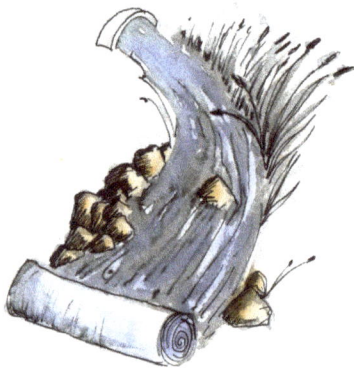

WHAT'S THE BOOK ABOUT?

The subject of this Barefoot Guide is 'generative leadership.' There are tons of books about leadership but few, if any, that deal with what it means to be a generative leader. Here, we use the word 'generative' to point us towards what we think matters most and to steer us all away from ego-inflating distractions of being "the leader." We don't want to be rude in the very first paragraph, but neither your ego nor ours needs any inflating! And the world certainly needs less ego-driven leaders.

The question then is, what kind of leadership is needed in these times? You've opened pages written by people who care about this question, deeply, and we invite you to walk with us to explore it further. And, even if you are just a little curious, stay with us for a while and see what the landscape reveals!

GIVING LIFE A CHANCE

We're guessing that you're reading for the same reason we've written: We want our lives to contribute to giving life a chance. Life! Something so mysterious and miraculous and almost impossible fully to appreciate. Life has given us the chance to be human with our ordinary, and yet extraordinary individual and collective capacities to think, to feel and to create. We are generative beings, given life and giving life.

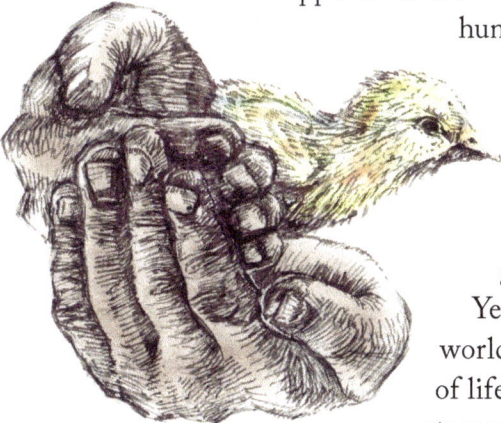

Yet the forces that drive the world, that determine our experience of life, seem to be quite the reverse, stemming from fear, cynicism, and hatred. We know, with no small frustration, nearing despair sometimes, that we are not doing the right things in the right way, even as time seems to be slipping away. Not just the time in our personal lives, but also time in the dynamics of fundamental systems on which human life itself depends: the cycles of the climate, the institutions of democracy and justice, the capacities we have developed over the millennia to talk to each other about what matters most, to be together now, on earth.

We are generative beings, given life and giving life

The typical response to our growing urgency is to learn more about fixing things—to grasp for one more book, podcast, video, seminar, degree or certification that promises just the formula for the leadership we need. Yet, yet, and yet … textbooks and practices that make for peace, mercy, and justice seem more elusive and distant than ever.

This book starts and thus ends very differently. It's not much about skills, techniques, or tools, but about a different set of capabilities. *We notice life* and we are *actively curious* about how our lives might be aligned with their ever-creating flow of possibilities. We are curious less about which terrible problem we should focus our effort upon (though we still notice those) and more on what life suggests is trying to happen among us, around us, and beyond us, and on how to release that energy. Life generates its next possibilities in a radically creative, almost playful way. We want to understand how it works and thus, how we might work with it and through it.

This kind of active curiosity is not abstract; we are guided by what we see life doing in the most hopeless situations. Even there we are curious about how life finds a way because we want our lives to help life find a way for the people, families, neighbourhoods and natural systems that we love. We write out of that urgent love to allow our minds, hearts, and hands to do better work.

Life generates its next possibilities in a radically creative, almost playful way

The one thing we are clear about is that we don't need to fight to fix things. Inevitably, paradoxically, tragically, that way too often strengthens the forces of fear and cynicism, however "right" it may feel. There are surely times when we have to forcefully defend what is human, but those are not enough. There are also more creative, life-giving ways.

Every single aspect of every corner of every human institution and network is in radical and dynamic change. We share the anguish of how some people's self-seeking ways and powers seem to be able to ride the waves of change while staying aloft on their privileges. But we feel less inclined simply to fight what we fear and much more inclined to see where the hidden flows of life are present and leading—so that we can spend our energy on crafting lives and roles that are worthy of what comes next. Some of us, tuned to the ancient faith traditions, sense a time between times and remember that we are urged to live confident lives built on what is coming. Our urgent love casts out fear.

Like you, we have been part of many discussions about leadership. These often assume that the work of leading institutions and networks is hard, needing ever more skills in planning and doing and speaking and, and, and ….

Yet, we are guided by something else. Early in our meetings, one of our authors, who is an environmental scientist, told the story of a river close to his home that had been canalized many years ago, lined with beds of concrete to control its occasional floods. More gutter than river, more concrete than flow, it became as stuck as any political conundrum. Nobody thought of it as alive or even capable of life anymore. But a brilliant and bold ecologist had the preposterous idea that the life of the river would restore its own possible flow if one bored some thoughtfully placed holes through the concrete—creating openings to give life a chance. (In Chapter 1 you can discover what happened next.)

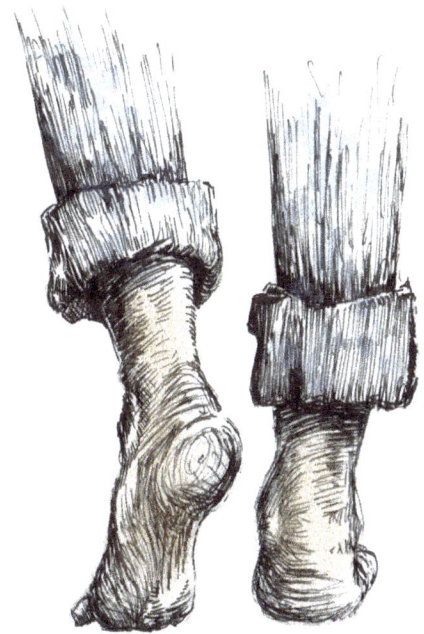

It takes less time to lay concrete than for the roots of old trees to find their way down into the soil below. But you don't need to tell a root how to find soil, and the effort to release life may be far less than it takes to bury it. And we must accept the reality of existing concrete and meet it's challenge even as we lament its existence. The story is rich in detail, both cautionary and hopeful; but it beckons us to work with living forces as partners. Any human neighbourhood is far more complex than any river, so we do not recommend letting the ecological metaphor do all the work. But perhaps it can relieve us of some of the over-anxious energy that tempts us to imperial and mechanistic solutions.

Leadership of complex human systems is more like drilling holes in the concrete to give life a chance than it is removing the concrete. A river is a river because it works with gravity, not against it. It took a bold ecologist—and patience—to punch the holes in a concrete channel, but then the river knew what to do. So too, human systems move naturally toward life; even, we are bold enough to say, toward mercy, justice, and love.

You don't need to tell a root how to find soil, and the effort to release life may be far less than it takes to bury it

OUR STORY IS NOT YOUR STORY

We have approached this process of writing about a more generative way of leading in the way that makes sense to us. We don't assume it all fits your context exactly. Your curiosity may bound from one idea to another in a different order, informed by your own life experience, your own urgent and very particular love of people and place. In fact, we are certain that your story is one we are missing.

So we hope you will take this offering of pages as an invitation to be part of a learning community that will simply not quit. We hope you will make us braver, en*courage* us, in taking the path toward life. Though we have a strong sense of the fragility and complicity of much that we have to deal with in our world right now, we do not yet know enough about the emerging patterns and systems that we are living into. How could we? Neither does any chick in any egg. It must feel brave to peck away at the shell, for what lies beyond is unknown. Yet any chick too timid to break its way through dies in the dark. Life drives us beyond our timid steps to find our way beyond our shell. As generative beings, we are courageous too!

We write of breaking through, of being broken open ourselves, of finding our way. The cracking is good news.

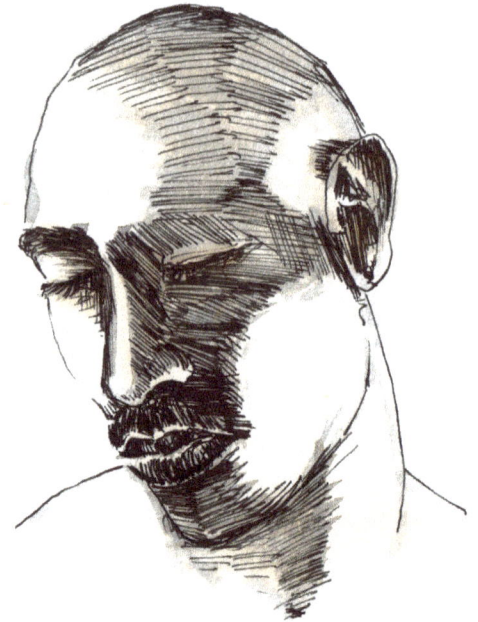

Any chick too timid to break its way through dies in the dark

REALITY CHECK

The contributors to this Guide come from a variety of places: Tanzania, Zimbabwe, South Africa, Norway, USA, Nicaragua, Guatemala, and Afghanistan. There are roughly two dozen of them. Each has rich experience in their home places and in other parts of the world, and all have confronted and had to deal with difficult or even dangerous times.

Though our particular, grounded identities are precious to us, we are drawn to live and act in leadership roles for the sake of all, no matter who they are or where they are finding their life or how they name themselves. Whether or not they are like us, we want to find our lives in contributing to theirs. We are moved by our love for the very particular communities and neighbourhoods and wild places we know as our own, and we hope our lives will lend a little of the nourishment they need to have a better chance for this and coming generations.

But we know that chance depends largely on the chances of the larger all-encompassing hopes on our tiny planet. Because we are tied with intimate bonds to a few, we follow those threads to the whole.

So our desire for our leadership to be generative will be fulfilled when this Barefoot Guide is co-owned in its intention and its use by people across the larger social divides that mark our neighbourhoods, our cities, our countries, and our humanity as such. That means a key question must stay in the foreground: Is my—our—leadership cognizant of those now disempowered, excluded and discriminated against? Is our aim to benefit those who are socially most distant from my social class, my gender, my 'race,' and the like? Is my leadership generative of the well-being of all?

This points to one of the biggest challenges of our time—the profound divisions, so easily manipulated for one or another self-interest, that not only harm us but also the planet we live on. So a reality check is necessary.

All the authors of this Barefoot Guide would be recognized as involved in some aspect of civil society, though some have links into government or business institutions. Most of us are rooted in the middle class rather than as part of the poor and excluded in our society. An awareness of the contradictions that deepen the divide places a special obligation on generative leaders and actors, wherever they originate.

Is my leadership generative of the well-being of all?

For example, in South Africa—home of several of the authors—"white" or "liberal" charity is deeply entrenched and usually seen by those who "give" as the means to improve or comfort those previously denied the vote. Those in receipt of this charity often argue that it is this that now impedes the realization of their dreams and hopes—a new colonization. "Enlightened" white South Africans have struggled with this assertion, sometimes rejecting it implicitly or explicitly for fear that it takes away the very basis of their ethos of helping those less advantaged than they are. Having grown up with a sense that they should take a lead and have the means (money, knowledge, education, experience, authority, or power) to do so, it's hard to do anything else.

All our efforts to change society into a better place, from whatever dominant social structure, must recognize this basic point. It entails 'standing back' when the natural instinct is to lead and 'show that you know better'. The South African freedom fighter, Steve Biko, who helped motivate so many other people to lead, was and remains the best exponent of this shift in modus. The challenge to achieve what is suggested here is tough. It requires a bridge that can be crossed where at the moment there is brokenness and a chasm that threatens to engulf us.

It may be almost too obvious to mention, but we are drawn to this generative way of living and leading at the very moment that drastic initiatives are required to save life on earth. Surely something more heroic, desperate and powerful is called for than a gentle word like "generative"? So many of the places we love are suffering a pox of despots, a riot of the rich trampling with glee as the forests fail and tundra melts. Surely we must fight!?

Yes and no. Yes, because we are not saying just accept or give in to those who do harm. No, because the deepest and most profound challenge is to nurture the seed, protect the sprout and give everything we have to the work and hope of generativity. We think that life has made it these dozen billion years or so just that way—by generating into every unlikely nook and cranny in the whole universe, betting everything on the forces of life finding their way.

The deepest and most profound challenge is to nurture the seed, protect the sprout and give everything we have to the work and hope of generativity

With that confidence, let us turn the page on our fears and lend ourselves to the ways of generative leadership. What could matter more? Why live otherwise?

This is the invitation of this Barefoot Guide on Generative Leadership. It is not an attempt to produce or teach a new model of leadership; it is the fruit of a diverse community of practitioners from around the world and from a diversity of contexts committed to exploring and learning together about what it means to participate in generative, life-giving and life-enhancing leadership. For us the work will continue long after the book is published but perhaps, in reading and entering into the flow of this river, you too will join us in discovering what it means.

IF WE SURRENDERED ...

FROM RAINER MARIA RILKE,
Book of Hours II

"If we surrendered
to earth's intelligence
we could rise up rooted, like trees.

Instead, we entangle ourselves
in knots of our own making
and struggle, lonely and confused.

So like children, we begin again...

to fall,
patiently to trust our heaviness.
Even a bird has to do that
before he can fly."

CHAPTER 1

RELEASING LIFE
Let the River Flow

CRAIG TALKS ABOUT A RIVER:

"Hot summer days at my home often include a walk down to the small river flowing through my community. It's an opportunity for me to cool my feet and for my dogs to splash, for the children to explore and collect tadpoles along the way. It's also a time for all of us to connect with the living organisms that exist in the river and to be reminded of life not captured or strangled by the brick, concrete and tar of the city.

The Liesbeek River flows through my neighbourhood in Cape Town, South Africa. In global terms it is more stream than river as it meanders for 9km from the eastern slopes of Table Mountain through suburbs and light industrial areas before joining the Black River and draining into the Atlantic Ocean.

For hundreds of years the river has been pivotal in the lives of those living near it. In precolonial times the Khoikhoi lived lightly along the banks as nomadic pastoralists with limited impact on the river system. After colonial settlement the Liesbeek was the first river in South Africa to be impacted by colonial agriculture and urbanization though life along its banks remained pivotal for its new inhabitants.

But the relationship with the river eventually changed. By the time I first moved into the area nearly two decades ago the river was no longer connected to life alongside it. It was a conduit for disease and a haven for crime, more drainpipe than river. Ugly and polluted the river area was largely avoided by the communities through which it flowed, disconnected from all the life around it and perhaps no longer even a river."

A RIVER BECOMES A CANAL

As the City of Cape Town grew, the area along the Liesbeek became increasingly occupied by residential and light industrial activity. Severe flooding events in the 1940s impacted on the people and suburbs along the river resulting in a decision to canalize sections of the river. Eventually around forty percent of the Liesbeek was canalized in the early 1950s.

WHAT IS A RIVER?

Rivers have played a key role across human history in the development of civilisations, with some of the world's first great civilisations emerging on the floodplains of the Euphrates and Tigris in the middle east, the Nile in Africa, the Indus in India, and the Huang in China. They provided routes for travel and transport across vast distances allowing for trade and the exchange of culture and ideas, and power for driving machinery and the generating of electricity.

Rivers are complex systems that are in constant change generating a wide variety of life and habitat in, around and below the water's surface. The visible flow of water above the ground is only a portion of the water flowing in the river and the water is but one element of the river. Rivers are living systems brimming with connections between what is happening underground, on the banks, and in the life around the water.

No two rivers are the same and each individual river changes significantly over time in response to its changing context and according to the seasons. The variation of flow across place and time is critical to the ongoing life and healthy functioning of rivers. Canalisation seeks to control and remove this variation and change in order to deal with the inherent risk of flooding, assuming that one component of the river can be isolated from the rest without fundamentally changing the nature of the river. But precisely this movement and change is what keeps the river alive and generative, healthy and functioning.

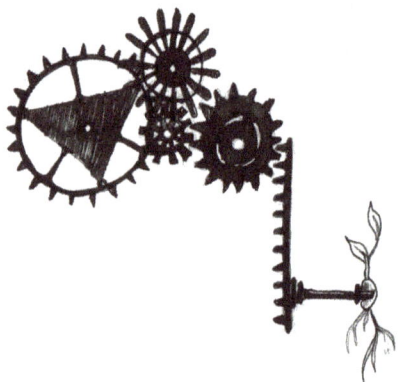

The decision to canalize the Liesbeek River reflected the industrial, mechanistic mindset of the age seeking to impose human order on nature's chaos. If rivers are simply the flow of water from one point to another then canals are more efficient at delivering water through the system, less messy and unpredictable and able to mitigate the damage caused by flood events. This "order" has been imposed on streams like the Liesbeek as well as immense rivers like the Mississippi River in the United States of America.

CRAIG:

"I am interested in the notion of leadership and the gift that good leadership can be to a community. As a high school teacher I participated in leadership development of students and as a community development practitioner I've become interested in social change and how leadership plays a role in this. Leadership as 'process and people' has the capacity to be life generating for those in a community system. In that way it's like a river; we can work with the flow of life or we can turn it into a canal."

CANALISED LEADERSHIP

Modern leadership practice has been deeply influenced by instrumental thinking. In this thinking whole systems can be broken down into constituent parts that can then be understood as independent of each other. The whole is assumed simply to be the sum of these parts largely ignoring how the connections between the parts impact the whole. Change is assumed to be a linear progression of cause and effect that can be analyzed, described and then replicated as universal best practice models across multiple contexts. Human order continues to be imposed on nature's chaos.

In this canalized approach to leadership, leaders have become risk managers as the uncertainty and ambiguity of social and organizational life undermines predictable and knowable future outcomes. Seeing life as a series of risks to be contained or problems to be solved, leadership is expressed through technical management skills, designing interventions, and controlling behaviour, all intended to deliver specific outcomes in the most efficient way possible.

Isolating a few visible tasks or people in the leadership process and separating them from the context in which leadership happens is much like isolating the above-ground flow of water from the rest of the river. It turns an inherently life giving and generative system into one devoid of life and often causing harm.

With the failure of leadership around the world—the product of accumulated years of canalized leadership—we face the question whether leadership can be generative of life, nurturing people rather that serving nameless systems.

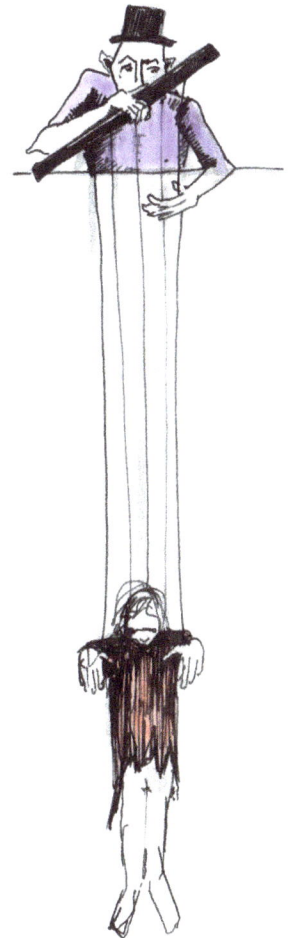

ENCOURAGING A RIVER BACK TO LIFE

CRAIG AGAIN:

"Around the time I moved into the neighbourhood alongside the Liesbeek River a small group of people had started meeting and formed the "Friends of the Liesbeek". They were beginning to imagine a different river, a river that could once again be a place of connection and life. They wanted to see the river brought back to life as a functioning and lifegiving system reconnected with the world."

FRIENDS OF THE LIESBEEK

The aim of the Friends of the Liesbeek (FoL) is to create an awareness of the importance of the Liesbeek as a green corridor in an urban setting and to rehabilitate, enhance, and conserve it and its environs.

The Friends of the Liesbeek began in 1991. Its first activities were river walks and cleanups, but today, the organization focuses more broadly on public awareness and education about the river environments.

The success of this volunteer group has been dependent on its mutually beneficial partnership with the City of Cape Town. FoL has adopted an unflinching, 'take-it-or-leave-it' approach to volunteerism that has allowed it to operate effectively on the same level as the government departments with which it deals. FoL's primary effort, the Liesbeek Maintenance Project – a large-scale river rehabilitation scheme – is reliant on the knowledge and support of the municipality.

The success of FoL makes a strong case for the potential of volunteer organisations and demonstrates that, in partnership with government, much can be accomplished. The key is to stand apart from, but work with government.

A secondary aim is to work together in a community of practice where we explore new ways of thinking from the knowledge and experiences of participants. This community of practice will include the knowledge and resources from various academic and professional bodies as well as from first-hand knowledge with community groups.

From - http://fol.org.za/about/

Canalization allows for uniform and predictable movement of water throughout a system. But the central feature of rivers is the flow of water, varying and changing constantly. This variation creates new conditions in the river and is itself influenced by change in other parts of the river.

The Friends of the Liesbeek saw that in order to bring the river back to life the variation of flow would need to be restored, the habitat and substrate diversity would need to be developed, and the growth of riparian and instream vegetation in the river would need to be encouraged. They began several small experimental actions to achieve this.

It all began with small actions of walking the banks of the river, cleaning up and planting plants. It meant looking behind and beyond the concrete and seeing instead places where life was present and able potentially to be nurtured back into abundance.

Trying to remove all the concrete was both unwieldy and unnecessary. Nature is capable of doing a lot of the work. So cylindrical holes, 70cm in diameter, were broken through the base of the canal structure in various sites and filled with rocks, reconnecting the above surface flow with ground water. This increased the substrate variation, created new habitats, and protected areas for when floodwaters moved through the system.

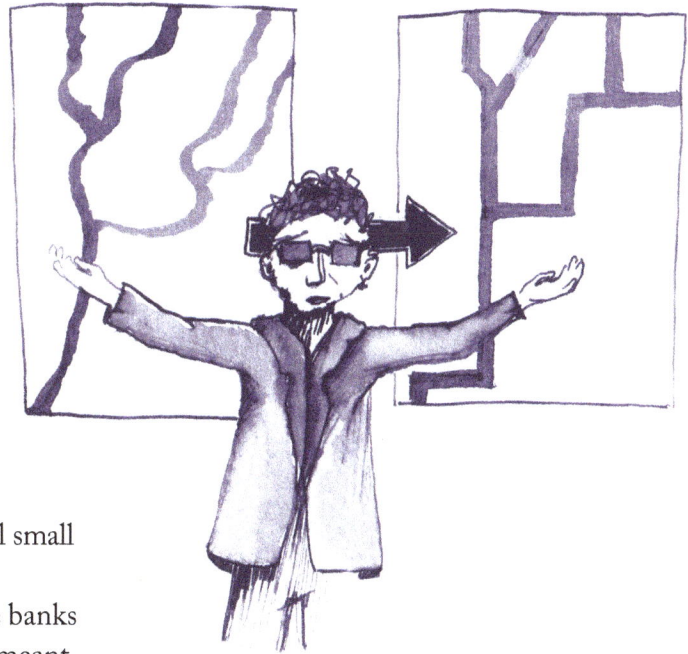

Breaking cylindrical holes through the base of the canal in various sites and filling them with rocks reconnected the above-surface flow with ground water

More structures and substrate were added, creating small rapids called riffles and runs along with small weirs. These small interventions generated variation in the flow of water from slow and sedate in deeper water, to fast and bubbling across rocks and down small waterfalls. More change happened as pebbles, rocks and sand were washed downstream, settling in different ways. The flow varied even more, creating greater diversity. An ever-changing evolving system began to emerge. Now different fauna and flora took advantage of the changing habitats, biodiversity increased, and the health of the river grew.

Rather than regularly clearing vegetation from the canal as in the past, the establishment and growth of riparian and instream vegetation was encouraged. The river was being significantly transformed, water quality improved, and new habitats emerged. New sandbanks, and trees started growing their roots again, pushing through cracks in the canal substrate, breaking it open further and so, increasing the general connectivity of the whole system.

These measures, along with careful monitoring and management of the system, have led to significant improvements in the quality of the river. Small shifts in initial conditions have released the river from its bondage. It is coming to life again for the first time in decades. Biologically the river is now considered fairly healthy with significant species diversity. The river is coming to life again and the communities through which it flows now see and experience it as a place of life and connection rather than a place to be avoided.

CRAIG'S EXPERIENCE:

"A place that I avoided is now a place to bring my children and dogs, cooling off on hot summer days and reconnecting with neighbours and with life. A place that restores and rejuvenates."

BRINGING LEADERSHIP BACK TO LIFE

Complex humans and human systems, like riverine ecosystems, cannot generally be understood by analyzing their constituent parts independently of each other. Forget this, or think you can deal simply with discrete parts of a human system and not the whole, and it's like assuming a river is simply the flow of water that can be separated from everything around it. Complex human systems are not characterized by linear cause and effect relationships that predict future behaviour in the system.

However, many leadership models approach human systems in precisely this way, promoting the idea that leaders can plan their way into a predictable and known future, removing uncertainty and ambiguity. But uncertainty and ambiguity are an essential mark of complex human systems, which are constantly adapting to what is happening within and around them.

Leadership practices that fail to understand and embrace this reality may become lifeless canals. Still, cracks will appear, something or someone will at some point break holes in the concrete, and life will find it's way through, leaving behind the leader who fails to see it coming.

The future cannot be definitively planned but the right conditions can be created to encourage emergent self-organization that will take the system in the desired direction, bringing leadership to life like a river emerging from the shackles of a canal.

The future cannot be definitively planned

Canalized leadership and its mechanistic, technical or instrumental view need to be disrupted, for the sake of life. Disconnections need to be turned into connections so that the energies of the people or group within which one leads are able to flow in ways that are life-giving for all.

When this is done in communities, organizations, institutions and generally in human groups, it inevitably unsettles the old order into which things have been contained and constrained. Then another kind of risk arises that has be to faced (not "managed" through control), the risk of more open space for new thinking and patterns to emerge that may challenge the desire for control.

This is hard for the leaders who have a strong need to exert their authority or positional power to move people and a system to their desired outcome. Rarely, when stories are told of leadership that has generated significant change, is the story told of the web of relationships and processes that enabled the change to happen. Rather the story attempts to locate the change in the work and giftedness of a single person.

ENCOURAGING VARIATION

So, we need to resist the temptation for a single, unified leadership model emerging—as if that is enough to match life. That's not what this Guide is trying to do. Rather, as the poem on the next page suggests, we need to learn to "release the bird," in ourselves and in others.

Give language to what is emerging

We know that we need a variety of solutions and even though we understand that some may fail, we are interested in as wide a range as possible of emergent approaches to leadership that are generative. Just as the growth of riparian and instream vegetation in a canal creates habitats and conditions for ongoing change so, too, ways must be found to encourage and nurture a wide variety of forms and practices of generative leadership held together by a few simple principles.

The building and creating of relationships across and between systems, enabling shared learning and practice, will further strengthen these ideas and generate new ideas and practices. As these new and novel approaches emerge there is a need for them to be interpreted and given meaning in a way that helps those in the system progress forward. Here the work is not to plan or design new models of generative leadership but to do the work of giving language to that which is emerging and describing it in a way that enables the ongoing emergence of the models.

Generative leadership emerges in multiple shapes and forms and some of these create significant life moving forward. Even those that fail provide the substrate for future action and learning. In pursuit of new generative leadership narratives, we must be willing to learn and fail our way into the future.

RELEASING THE BIRD

BY MOSI KISARE

Interlude: Boy in doubt…but they wait!

And they wait

It is the bird trapped in my hands

Waiting,

Until I let it fly

A rare gift in my hand,

that, says my father, I must let go.

I launch the bird out from my open hands

and watch the joy of flight and power gained in freedom.

Tossed out of a small boys' hands,

the trapped creature set free,

Mirror of the gift of my spirit.

A blessing to my soul.

A_n_d_ _t_h_e_y_ _w_a_i_t_…_

It is the ferry crew, pulling,

leaning back to launch a forward path,

urging me on with song.

Go on, find the new land,

across the big river and blue mountains.

I listen to their gritty music,

bearing the sound of drudgery.

Like mysterious guardians of my journey,

they sang of departures and arrivals.

I felt wronged.

The whole world had conspired against a small boy.

The river is deep and dark.

My heart is pumping with fear.

I am confused.

Why must I leave my parent's home?

They all want me dead! I know.

A_n_d_ _t_h_e_y_ _w_a_i_t_…_

It is the cows in the homestead Kraal,
The only company for a small boy left alone in a
strange home,
Waiting for me to act.
Their glaring stares urge me on. Gooo!
This prison is not for you.
I run.
Urged on by the prophetic gaze of a cow,
the cosmic wisdom of a humble gathering.
The celebrated new home now a bad memory,
I trace the path by which my father had guided me
to this place.
There is another river to cross, but no ferry crew.
Now I hear the murmurs of the river, and the
whistling wind.
I run.
Carried by extraordinary energy and agility.
Away I go. Lost, but there is a destination.
This is my first act of rebellion.
The river has become my own story.
I cross.
I have found my path.

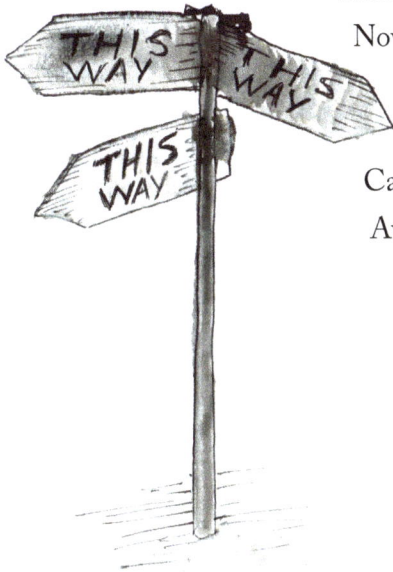

CHAPTER 2

POISONING THE RIVER

Life under threat

A healthy river teems with vitality, offering abundant life, as long as we respect it. But when it is diminished, poisoned, and threatened by neglect, over-exploitation and abuse, it degenerates and even becomes deadly. We see leadership heading the same way in many parts of our world. Degenerate leadership is becoming normalized—something we are supposed to accept as natural or inevitable— with careless leaders promoting unjust, self-serving, and intentionally harmful ends. In this chapter we focus on what diminishes or poisons leadership, and look at some ways of responding to the stress this causes.

LEADERSHIP FOR LIFE IN THE FACE OF DEATH

The word "river" usually brings to mind healthy images of water flowing below tree-lined banks, fish darting around, children swimming, people relaxing, or perhaps waterfalls worth pictures. They are life-giving, but … they can also kill. Our dear colleague Steve De Gruchy, who would have written for this guide, died in flooded rapids while tubing with his son in February, 2010. We wonder what he would have said about rivers as a metaphor for leadership. We know that his last words to his son were: "Go on without me, I'll be alright!" Maybe that's about right in terms of counsel.

In 1969 the Cuyahoga River caught fire in downtown Cleveland, burning bridges and buildings all along its bank. Enough oil and poison had been dumped into it to burn. This weirdly iconic incident ignited the modern environmental movement in the United States. It was at least the 18th time the river flamed, and not the worst, but something about the moment gave power to the idea. People of every political view agreed that rivers should not catch fire. Today the river is still far from its natural flow but forty-four kinds of fish are back in the improving waters.

Cuyahoga means 'twisted'. Like it's name, it is witness to the long, twisting nature of change in complex community systems. Generative leadership never happens at the beginning of any process. It always engages a river of history already in motion, carrying what flows down out of the surrounding social watershed. Most social phenomena are shaped through currents that have carved their banks over many generations. Even the tiny and relatively young Cuyahoga dodges its way around hills formed by the last glaciers, only 10 thousand years ago. The mighty ones such as the Zambezi, Congo, Niger or Mississippi flow in much deeper ancient channels.

What can we learn here? What flows in or around us are the social realities of the places we work in and live in. To pay serious attention to these realities, with humility, is the first lesson for generative leaders.

We also learn that while you cannot change gravity, or the direction of the river, we can stop poison from entering the stream. Poison is not gravity; it is not inevitable. Once it is in the water, it must flow out and away. So, it does not have to flow in, but if it does, the forces of nature can help it flow out. A generative leader sees the poison that flows through an organization or community but treats it as a living phenomenon, pays attention to all that connects to it, and helps the system find its way of cleaning and healing itself.

The Cuyohoga shows the complexity of this, but also the healing possibilities resulting from people who form a common bond, illuminated by science about problems and pathways. Taking them on we become part of the living system of the social watershed, keenly sensitive to what is uphill that affects us and what is downhill that affects the next. The key generative step is to make all of that conscious, to bring it to mind and then to action, using all available tools to raise and change consciousness. For long it was unthinkable that the Cuyohoga would be anything but toxic. But then poets, singers, preachers and eventually politicians found their voice, like Randy Newman, who sang,

Cleveland city of light city of magic
Cleveland city of light you're calling me
Cleveland, even now I can remember
'Cause the Cuyahoga River
Goes smokin' through my dreams

A whole generation of people began the change. Generative leadership isn't something a single person called "leader" does to a group of people called "followers." Generative leadership isn't the list of tricks and techniques one applies to a system, organization or network to make it do something against the forces of social gravity. It can't perform unnatural acts. And it can't get adults to do things they aren't willing to do. But generative leaders can work with gravity to let the poison flow out. With eyes wide open, one who is part of the system can help the social possibilities become conscious, choose-able and do-able.

It would be a happier and shorter story if generative leaders only had to deal with rocks and water. But social poisons are not so natural. One group's poison that serves up daily dread is another group's profit and daily bread. The Cuyohoga burned because factories were built on its banks; toxic effluent could simply be dumped and left as someone else's problem. Nobody thought of the river as anything other than as God's gift of gravity.

One group's poison that serves up daily dread, is another group's profit and daily bread

Social problems of a more subtle, yet deadly, nature are just like that. Privileges, like river banks, hold in place the easy patterns of abuse, domination, and extraction that seem naturally convenient—to those benefiting from the relationship. How could it be other? Until one day the river burns.

We stand on the bank watching as our beautiful and bewildering world burns, shaking our heads, wondering where we are headed as a planet, as a people, as a species. We cringe as we see all around us unbridled profiteering and the inequality and poverty it spawns, the awful and endless wars, climate change, racism and bigotry, the choking pollution…. We know that these are not isolated things but deeply intertwined consequences of a chaotic global economic and political system. We are worried. Many of us are in despair, immobilized by the seeming impossibility of doing anything about this.

Our democratic political systems, better labeled *democrazy*, which we once hoped would enable peace, justice and prosperity for all, have become illogical and dysfunctional, rupturing the social fabric that brings us together as civilized human beings. Through ingenious manipulation, our social media has quite simply deceived the public into voting for scoundrels. If we do vote it is often for those politicians we dislike or distrust the least. We look to our national and global leaders for answers, for hope that they can see what we see and are working together on a plan, but what we see is a gallery of fools playing to the markets and the fears of the voters, seemingly in the thrall of broken economic and political systems that they have given up trying to change. Not all of them, but so many that our heads are hurting from the shaking.

Are we, as a species, incapable of living peacefully and equitably with one another, despite our differences and diversity? Are we lesser beings than we have imagined, uncaring of those beyond our families, tribes or nations. Are we, in our DNA, competitive and aggressive creatures who must win or lose, whose highest purpose on earth is to make money, consume stuff and pursue pleasure, regardless of the long-term consequences for the planet and future generations? If we take our cue from the leaders of the world today, it would appear so.

"According to Oxfam's analysis, last year 26 people owned the same wealth as the 3.8 billion people who make up the poorest half of humanity, down from 43 people the year before."

- Public Good or Private Wealth
Oxfam Briefing Paper, January 2019[1]

There is only one river in which we all live, from which we all drink

Let's look a little deeper. What really lies behind the behaviour of our national and global leaders? Is it greed or fear or love of power? It may be. Perhaps they are greedier, more fearful or lustful of power than most – but they are human after all and who knows, if we took their places we may soon become like them. But this cannot explain the sheer wanton immorality of what they do, the compromises and deals they make to preserve a system that they and we know is driving us over a cliff!

What we see behind all these "qualities" is something far scarier: *a deep and dangerous cynicism about life itself,* a carelessness for life, for each other, a disregard for our extraordinary human capacities for love, for creativity, for the joy of family and community, for the bountiful magnificence of earth and nature.

If Steve De Gruchy reminded us with his death that rivers are dangerous, he also taught us that we all live downstream: *There is only one river in which we all live, from which we all drink.*

ON NOT BEING OVERCOME

The community of thought and practice that finds voice in the Barefoot Collective is a network of networks, extending far and deeply into neighborhoods trying to create their way to lives of decency. It is the nature of these networks to be widely dispersed, highly particular and different, yet resonating to very similar dynamics.

Nothing is more common than the distress we feel by the overarching rip tide pulling our work back into the deep and cold water of injustice. Our best efforts seem so often to be minor, overwhelmed by the powerful currents. Even those of us working in relative safety and privilege can read the data and do the math that mocks our hopeful scenarios.

We are not comforted by happy chirps of optimism.

We cannot trust a counsel from someone who does not seem to understand the tragic caughtness of our stuck processes.

We do not wish a way of leadership rooted in naiveté unlikely to survive the first hard winds.

We don't want to just feel better; we wish to do better.

Here the great traditions guide us in a way counter to the happy technologists of our day. The great traditions were all born of suffering, seeking a way to pass through and not just around the things that happen in life that stop and break us; the child in pain, the young dad with cancer, the village swept by flood. The traditions offer up the tools of lament that invite us into the depth of the experiences of grief and loss. And then they invite us to move through them and onto the work of life that lies beyond. Not all of us may share those traditions, but we all sense the wisdom of not hurrying past the negative, especially if we wish to serve the positive, the works of mercy and justice.

All humans are part of the same conscious species, but not all in the same way. The hope, then, is to move toward a common consciousness about what matters most. The generative leadership that holds the hope of the future may be caught, contained and held tight in systems and by things they cannot control, but their consciousness can reach across the cold waters.

In the early 1980s during the height of the South African Apartheid state's attempt to secure the divide between Blacks and Whites, a cartoon strip in a local paper pictured an alien spacecraft landing in a white suburban garden in Sea Point, Cape Town. Confronting the black gardener, the alien says: "Take me to your leader!" The gardener raises his arm and points across the sea to Robben Island where Nelson Mandela was imprisoned.

Mandela was a "heroic" leader, but that's not the point. What he represented and we look up to was *our* humanity, our deep and abiding *capacity for leadership*, visible in him but, as he himself saw and said, present as potential in every one of us who is human.

Our astonishing imaginations and ingenuity, our capacity for compassion and kindness, for cooperation and co-creativity, and *for doing the right thing*, is locked up somewhere across an expanse, yearning for release. Despite the years of hurt done to him and many of his people, the hope he called forth lay there. In us.

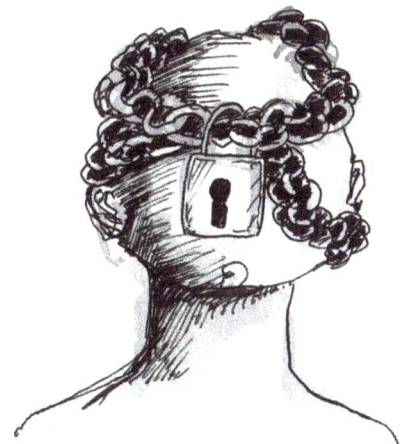

In each of us is a deep and abiding **capacity** *for leadership*

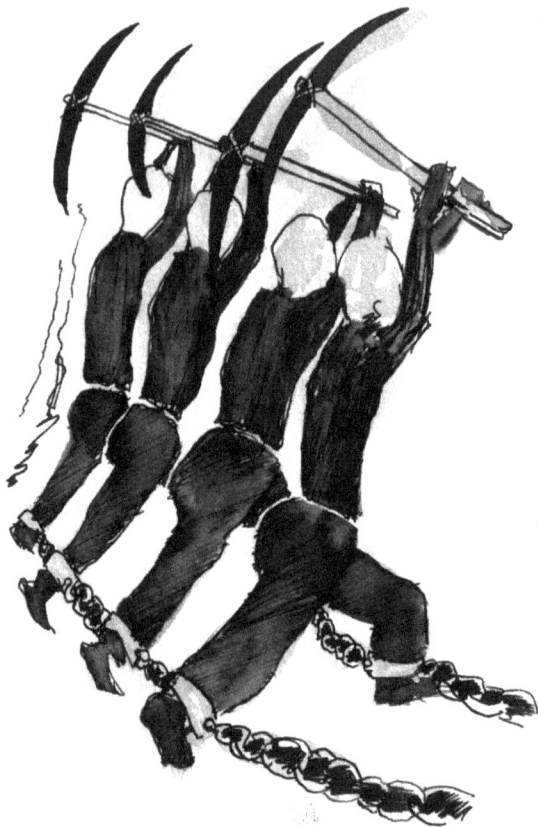

RELEASING ENERGY THROUGH LAMENT

A lament or lamentation is a passionate expression of grief, often found in music, poetry or song form. It can also be a part of a formal mourning process, and may result in wailing, moaning or crying. Lamentation dates way back to the earliest centuries and crosses almost all cultures.

It was part of the blues in the US South: songs of slaves and then freed slaves and poor sharecroppers of all colours in the mean Delta who sang to rid their souls of pain from unremitting stress of discrimination, violence, injustice, then poverty, while still tolling away in horrendous circumstances. In all the holy texts, lamentation is a way to release pain, "with a witness" to make the ritual more potent and useful.

WE FEEL IT ...

We know that our world needs healing. During our first Writeshop for this Barefoot Guide, we held our own lamentation ceremony.

Many recent events had happened to shake our hearts and souls. 60 people were killed and over 400 wounded by a systematic psychopathic shooting at a concert in Las Vegas; in the aftermath of Hurricane Harvey, Irma and then Maria, friends still hadn't heard after weeks from parents living high in the mountains of Puerto Rico; one of us heard that three medical colleagues in Nicaragua had drowned in their car trying to reach a community in need during a storm; another that family members of three different friends had committed suicide in the last month; and still another that 30 young people from their town had died from opioid abuse in the previous months.

And so we gathered together around a large fire under a bright moon surrounded by the Fynbos of the mountainside near Cape Town in South Africa, sang songs of lamentation, and spoke our sorrows into the fire.

In too many places, we see increasing hostility and divides among political parties and groups, hate crimes, corrupt high level leadership, a widespread move away from public integrity in favour of lies and worse, and megalomaniac national leaders tweeting like insipid school boys when the stakes are nuclear.

Such things bear down upon us. They build cumulative trauma, sorrow and grief across the world. Besides anything else, we need healing rituals to release that grief, sorrow and pain.

Offering a lamentation ritual to communities that have suffered these traumas is important, as none are immune. Families, individuals and communities need a way to absorb these tragedies and find a way to release that sorrow, grief, and painful energy.

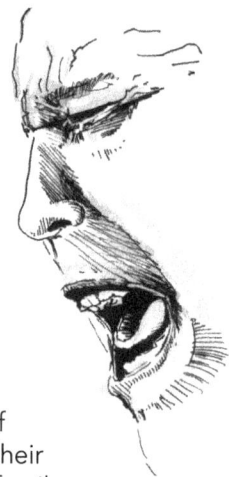

Lament is *not* complaining or passively mourning anything. It's releasing the energy that is otherwise blocked or repressed so that we can act again, but now with deeper insight and greater sensitivity.

Here ritual helps. It offers "safe containers" for allowing our hurt and our hope to be expressed openly with others. It unblocks the trauma and gives us energy to go forward. When done well it can play a valuable role in sustaining the generative powers of leadership. It requires sensitivity, being aware that people have different ways of dealing with hurt and anticipating hope, without peer or social pressure.

There are many ways to create a container for a lamentation ritual. It may include but doesn't have to include aspects of any structured religion but it needs to be a comfortable space for all who are there.

What could a Community of Practice around Lamentation Rituals look like?

CREATING A LAMENTATION RITUAL

Here are some ideas and basic elements that any local group could use to create their own rituals. Many cultures have very strong traditions in this area, as do most structured religions. One could incorporate elements of all these groups without being locked into any one tradition or structure.

Fit it to the setting and make sure it's appropriate to the group present yet still as inclusive as possible. Honour all who are present and let each participate as they wish— don't exert any social pressure to conform. Create it together, make it local, meeting culture and context.

SOME "MINIMUM SPECIFICATIONS" FOR RITUALS OF LAMENT

SETTING – Outside in nature may be best, but wherever it is, it should be a neutral space, not one that sets people apart. It should go beyond any particular faiths so that all will be welcome, including those of no particular faith tradition.

MUSIC – Use it for contemplation. The group could sit or stand in a circle to signify unity, and think or pray about the sorrows/grief/tragedies they wish to release while the music plays. All should be silent (though crying or wailing may happen). If you use songs, try ones that evoke grief or sorrow and can be universally understood. Here's one example of a song of sorrow, "Too Many Martyrs," by Phil Ochs, a 1960's civil rights activist.

Too Many Martyrs

(For Medgar Evers)

Too many martyrs and too many dead

Too many lies, too many empty words were said

Too many times for too many angry men

Oh, let it never be again.

NAMING THE PAIN – Create a time for calling out the names of those lost or hurt or the events themselves in some way, naming the trauma or grief.

AT-ONE-MENT – Use some iconic, sensory way of becoming at "one with" one another spiritually, like drumming, chanting, wailing, etc., with a focus on allowing time for this to happen.

MOVEMENT AND DANCE – A way to allow people literally to "get it out of their system" and release emotion (a version of "gnashing of teeth and ripping our garments") is to use bodily movements like free dance or movement in a circle.

LETTING GO – Build in a moment where people could bring an iconic symbol of someone or something they lost to "bury" and release or burn or let go of in some other way. Even a wish or a prayer or a statement can be written on a piece of paper and buried or burned.

HOPE/REBIRTH/RESURRECTION – This is a time for participants to commit to undertake some task in their life or work to commemorate loss and grief, a way of "going forward" (such as leading a similar lamentation ritual in their own neighbourhood or group, reach out to a family with a loss, etc.). This time could include music, walking in a circle at the end, passing the peace, whatever signifies solidarity and instills hope.

BENEDICTION – A blessing from someone in the group, or a poem, (e.g., Maya Angelou's *Still I Rise*), followed by a last piece of motivating music to reflect moving forward.

CELEBRATION – This could be in the form of sharing a meal together, creating a group artwork, expressing gratitude, etc.

POST-RITUAL STEPS – A Lamentation Ritual can't be just a "one-off" event; it's not any kind of "easy solution. "Sorrow often bubbles up in surprising ways and times. It's an ongoing process to which the group could commit themselves through further communication and interaction around shared goals. Any meaningful lamentation ritual should release energy that is now ready to be released into the world. For example, participants may decide to do something about better mental health or combatting substance abuse, sharing ways of helping build resiliency in communities, confronting corruption and the misuse of power at local level, doing advocacy work about ill-treated children, joining in initiatives around climate change, or any number of possibilities that will be determined by their context.

INTEGRATING HURT AND HOPE
Power for Social Action

We know from experience that hurt and hope are not separate parts of our life. They flow into and affect each other. Both are real. We can try to ignore them. Or live only in hurt, which is merely despair; or only in hope, which is simply naïve.

If we pay attention, however, we notice that *unjust or unfair hurt*, when it is noticed and voiced, becomes subversive. It shows up what is going on and asks for action. We also notice that *hope evokes resistance*. It no longer accepts that things as they are, have to stay as they are.

A generative leader will pay attention to both hurt and hope together, recognizing that they can be integrated into meaningful action that is capable of reducing the reality of hurt and unleashing the power of hope. Here's a diagram that helps us visualize this dynamic relationship of hurt and hope in any actions we take.

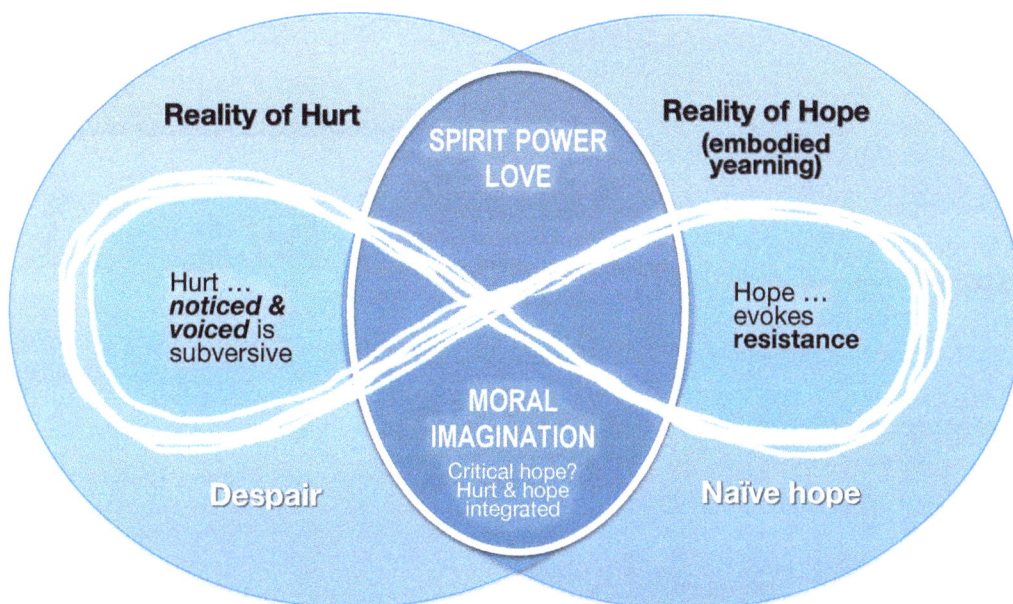

(Based on the work of Walter Brueggemann)

Our action takes place as a *lemniscate movement*—two loops that continually move back and forth between two centres. One centre is hurt which, suppressed, produces despair, but when noticed and voiced, is subversive and able to help us see where change is needed, whether in our organizations or communities or even our families. The other centre is hope, which, treated as mere optimism, is naïve, but when rooted in reality, evokes change in what needs to change or resistance to what prevents it.

We flow in and out of these realities, gathering energy and motion as we grasp and pay attention to the space between the overlapping realities of hurt and hope (the centre of the diagram). It's what happens in this middle space that is most crucial. It's here that people experience themselves in the midst of hurt, brutality, confusion or potential despair but also as able to find sparks (even bonfires!) of hope, connection and joy.

This is what animates them. This is the place of power and agency. What fuels and guides us is our moral imagination—our capacity to take responsibility for our hurt *and* hope to see what is in the world, what ought to be in the world, and to choose to act accordingly.

Becoming fully aware of this is important for a generative leader. It enables us to foster awareness, in ourselves, in other people, in communities, and in larger systems, of the power that exists in that centre, the "both-and" space. It helps us make this powerful space visible. When people are able fully to be aware of how both hurt and hope are operating in their experience and when they have the freedom and space to name them and draw on them in their work, there is agency and there is power.

FAILING FORWARD TOGETHER AT THE INTERSECTION OF HURT AND HOPE

Some things that poison the river of our life together involve systemic, structural forces and patterns of power. They often feel beyond what we can tackle.

Yet, just as supposedly hard riverbanks are always changing with the force of the flow, we know these forces and patterns are all a consequence of human actions. They are not impossible to change with other kinds of human action.

Leaders have a choice about why they lead and what for. They too can poison the river depending on how they act and with what intention. Just as the life of a river can be suppressed by canalizing it in concrete, so too leadership can be exercised to "colonize"—impose suffocating control over—the spaces that are necessary for life to emerge. Such a *corruption of leadership* can permeate even the 'do-good' industries or projects and programmes that end up really *complicit* in the professionalization and abstraction that canalizes life.

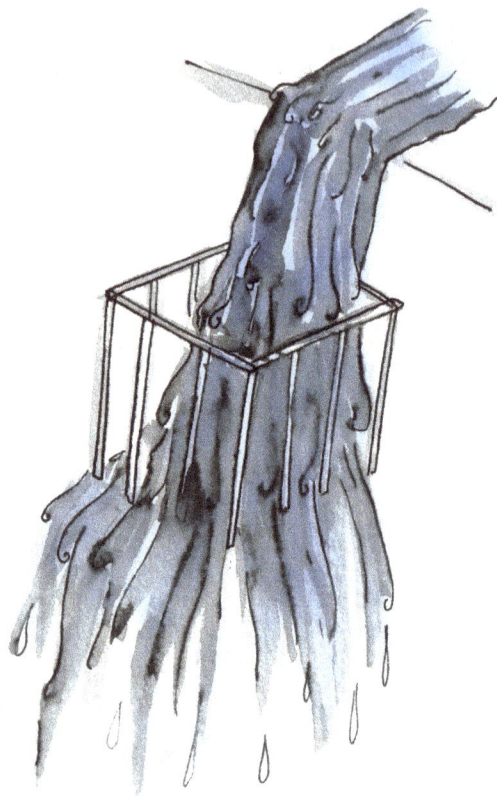

We are all capable of being complicit in many ways, of practicing what we can call *degenerative leadership*, when we fail to acknowledge and own our entanglement in the structures and patterns of power that diminish or harm the life that strives to emerge. Generative leadership does not shy away from probing the extent to which this may be the case in anything it does.

Generative leaders recognize that it is more likely than not that we will fall back on poor leadership behaviours or make mistakes--and build in ways to course correct. They are not afraid to acknowledge failure, and embrace it as a natural part of growth. They see failing forward as a norm, both in their leadership and in their work.

Somava, one of our authors, has thought about this a lot. Here she shares her story and some insights that help to think about this productively …

THOUGHTS ON 'FAILING FORWARD'

Over the last six months, my entire life has been upended, turned inside out, revealed to be my worst nightmare—one I have been staving off for over a decade. My heart feels betrayed and broken—by a person I knew better than to trust yet chose to put my faith in over and over again, because of my stick-with-it-ness—my cherished belief that there is always a solution, that you don't give up on people, that if you're strong enough and brave enough and creative enough and persistent enough, you will find a solution.

At its heart, I realized that although I teach about failing forward fast, and embrace it in my work, I had failed to embrace this practice in my own life—and as a result, had tolerated putting my child and myself in a situation that was harmful for us for over a decade, trying out solution after solution against all hope. It took a profound life-threatening crisis to finally make me realize that I was fighting for someone and something I never had the power to heal.

Those of us who are activists and change agents are prone to hope. We are, at our best, resilient when faced with adversity. We get right back up when we're knocked down, find the creative solution, garner the forces. In leading change, my strength has always come from being like water—I can almost always see a way through, around, over or under the problem. I am creative, strategic, able to see processes rise and emerge; I can almost always reframe a situation to a place of possibility, no matter how difficult. It is one of my gifts, part of what makes me a generative leader.

Sometimes you simply have to let go of something!

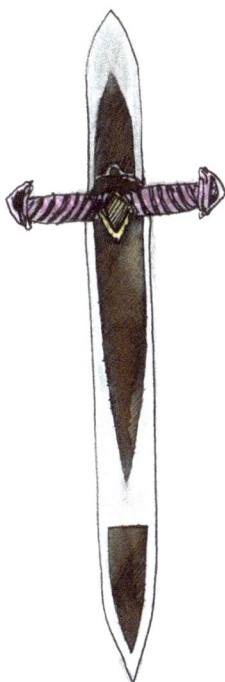

The sword edge of the gift that I am learning is that I sometimes stay in situations that are bad for me for far too long because I believe I can create a new possibility. In business school, they teach you that you should know your BATNA before you go into a negotiation—your *best alternative to a negotiated agreement* (BATNA). Once you go below your BATNA, you should walk away because there is a better alternative. I have often gone below my BATNA at great harm to myself personally and professionally—to continue to advance an initiative toward its goals.

At times, this has paid off. It has helped to keep a transformation going long enough for it to take deep root—roots that cannot easily be destroyed, resulting in deep sustainability. At times, it has led me to let go of things too late—often at great cost to myself.

How do we know when to persevere, when to learn fast and fail forward, and when to declare failure and move on?

Here are just a few practical tips:

If you're wondering about whether or not you should persevere, whether you should accept that you have failed and should now move on, then you probably need to consider it seriously. Because we are predisposed to not giving up easily, we need to pay extra attention when our inner teacher—that voice inside us—begins to speak up about this.

If you keep hitting your head against the same problem over and over again and all that's happening is that you are getting a bleeding and bruised head, then you almost certainly need to step back and consider a different approach.

If you feel yourself disappearing—if you are losing who you are or worse, what you believe in, as you try to accommodate to the situation—then you need to step back and question the situation.

If you have a sense of "déjà vu" about the situation—it looks uncomfortably familiar to a different scenario you were in that you don't want to repeat—then you probably need to take a step back. We tend to repeat our mistakes.

If you feel like you are lost and don't know where you are in the process anymore—then you probably need to go back up to the mountaintop to get a clearer view.

CHAPTER 3

THE RIVER'S JOURNEY
Re-authoring the World

A river journeys through mountains, forests, plains, villages, towns and cities, down to the freedom of the sea. Whether under threat from the toxic waste of industry, destructive developments, human neglect, or even nature itself, the river carries on to its destination, its end.

As rivers change through different landscapes, so generative leadership changes to flow through the situations it faces along the way, adapting and responding to meet the needs of people, organisations and communities, or the demands of society at large. However, like a life-giving river, generative leaders pursue the ends of a just, caring, and fulfilled life, regardless of the landscape. How do we think of these ends?
To what ends do you lead? That's what this chapter explores.

RE-AUTHORING THE WORLD

The world is not what it could be. Looking around much is amiss: frenetic and superficial relationships, little respect for crucial values and virtues, impatience, aggression, disconnection, inequality, exclusion and dispossession.

> 'There is a crack in everything. That's how the light gets in.'
> – Leonard Cohen

We have allowed others, who care little for life, to cynically impose their narratives on the world, authoring it in their own careless image. We have allowed them to squeeze out the space for genuine, generative human connection, reducing it to exchanging polarizing tweets or entertaining emojis. Worse, we have normalized and internalized those narratives without question, inhibiting other possibilities, real alternatives.

These are leadership narratives which canalize the rivers of our lives and interactions, excluding all but taken-for-granted ideas, beliefs and understandings, moving people along rigid, stagnant channels towards someone else's goals and mission, blocking out what is alive and life-giving.

We don't need to be stuck and trapped in the mess of the world. We don't have to allow others to determine the right way to lead. We don't need to buy a limited vision of leadership that restricts what we can see, to tell us what is worth paying attention to.

We don't have to accept the idea of "best practices" that seldom pay attention to the life that is emerging in communities everywhere and do not connect to the life force of the local reality.

We don't need to use profit-based notions of 'performance' to judge and assess ourselves or others, to determine how leaders and people are rewarded, affirmed and applauded.

We can write our own narrative of life and leadership that is humanizing, caring, conscious, generous and generative. We can re-author the world.

This requires our agency and authorship. It requires us to see, participate in and engage with the world in a new way. It demands that we refrain from seeing the world as static but, rather, as constantly becoming and renewing. It means taking responsibility for the ongoing renewal and co-creation of the world with a future filled with possibilities and choices.

Our responsibility is to be authors and co-authors of a world that celebrates what is life-giving, knowing that we cannot determine what will happen but that we can determine why and how we will act.

This includes re-writing our understanding of leadership. Against the hard-hearted, harsh and tired world of the early 21st Century we will do so consciously, deliberately and intentionally, with as much discipline and intellectual energy as we would give to anything.

What does this mean? At least this: helping people become unstuck in unhelpful narratives that do not take them forward; seeing the world as an ongoing conversation about creating or supporting new, emergent, generative possibilities; seeking local solutions built on existing capacities appropriate to what is right and good for that particular situation; being in service of each other, rather than aiming for gain.

Above all, it means living out of a different future that has a moral vision, nurturing leadership that rests on a view of authority that comes not from a position or an accreditation, not from power, control, manipulation and prestige, but from our understanding of a responsibility for creating a more human world for those we are called to serve and, ultimately, for all—informed by a vision for justice and equality in the world where every person counts and no-one is simply seen as a means to an end but are the end in themselves.

We can re-author the world

Leadership is about caring for people in a dignifying manner

Leadership should be about the people, caring for them in a way that is dignifying. Unafraid to face the cracks in the shadow side, it is generative leadership that understands that it is through the cracks that the light streams through. It is where we become weavers of conversations that invite and honour the narratives of the people and draws them into processes of co-creation and collective meaning making.

It is where we are guided by a careful curiosity, slow to judge others, wary of fixing things for them, generous in listening, open to surprise and delight, deeply appreciative of the uniqueness of people, ready to nurture them as primary authors of their story, showing deep respect for their humanity. It means cultivating practices that come from a place of not knowing rather than from a place of knowing.

Our humanity and the humanity of others become the coordinates that guide everything we do.

FOR WHAT ENDS DO WE LEAD?

Jim, one of our authors, had a conversation with his friend Doug M.[1] In their dialogue they explore the idea that, more than any skills or charisma, at the heart of generative leadership is the question of "ends"; of why we are leading, what motivates our leadership deep down, what shapes the crucial decisions we make. Of our most profound actions. Of the ends we serve with our life.

[*Jim*] So, let's talk a bit about "ends." I think to understand this, it helps to think about "means." We have many *means* (ways) to do things. This includes our skills, techniques, methods, even our personal gifts or talents.

[*Doug*] Yes, they are important, but they tell us *nothing* about the ends that guide us, about our most important intentions in leading anything, about what we are aiming at ultimately. And that's really crucial.

[*Jim*] Some 'ends' are clear enough, of course. If I lead a non-profit organization that wants to help educate children or AIDS orphans cope with the loss of their parents, then I serve those ends.

[*Doug*] OK, nothing wrong with that, but all ends or purposes like these, however valid, are inherently narrow. They serve only limited *organizational, or institutional, imperatives (necessities) and obligations (duties).*

[*Jim*] And I guess are not necessarily generative.

[*Doug*] They could be, but they might just as easily not be, especially when these limited needs outweigh or even damage broader needs. Think of a health care system. Obviously, its main end is the health of those it serves. But what if the system serves only those who can afford to use it? It may offer world-class medical science to some individuals but, because too many people can't afford it or access it, does the health profile of its surrounding community really ever change?

[*Jim*] Uh-huh, generative leaders, of any kind of institution or organization, would understand themselves as part of a wider whole. A generative leader asks questions like: "So who *does* this organization and institution really serve? Why is it doing its work in the first place? How can it avoid serving only some and not other people who might need it?"

> '*What I really want to do is be a representative of my race, of the human race*'
>
> Maya Angelou, 2013, from *George Stroumboulopoulos Tonight*, shortly before her death in May, 2014 at age 86.

[Doug] Yet it seems that most leadership training teaches skills, techniques, methods, and theories of leadership but not about the ends we serve beyond what we are expected to achieve in a specific role or task.

[Jim] That's a challenge. You can be a great leader for completely the wrong ends, like a drug lord whose gang members respect him and to whom some young people are attracted to and want to follow. He may be a leader, but a *generative* leader? Absolutely not!

[Doug] OK, point made, but we aren't really talking just about criminals. Very good people can also lead for ends that may not be bad in themselves but are *simply too limited.* Positional leaders tend to see everything in terms of "what's good for me or my group or my organization." That's OK in its place, but it means never asking how what you do or decide fits into what's good for everyone else. It's a kind of self-interest that determines the ends.

[Jim] Sure, though of course self-interest isn't always bad. It's *part* of being human, sometimes it's even *necessary* when others seek to harm you. Then 'self-interest' in protecting one's life and dignity could be vital.

[Doug] Yes, but it's *only part* of what it means to be human; when it becomes dominant it can do a lot of harm. Self-interest isn't enough for truly generative leadership. *The issue is whether and to what extent you go beyond mere self-interest.* Though no-one forces us to, we can do that, and many people do. That's also part of being human, and its vital!

[Jim] Then generative leadership is not just about making things work better or people feel better. You can have all the expertise, personal charisma, or the right skills do a good job and still lead for limited, self-interested, or maybe even bad ends.

[Doug] Exactly. The focus is on what we intend in leading—what we 'will' or want to bring into being. *It's about the basic orientation out of which we live and act!* Skills, expertise, character, talents, they may all be useful, even important, for some ends but the key question is: how large are those ends, how encompassing? Which ends are truly generative and guide everything we do?

[Jim] Fundamentally, the real end of generative leadership is about enabling us all to develop our capacities to unfold fully as human beings. Of course, lots gets in the way of this that we have to confront and deal with. A person who was a generative leader is Steve Biko, a founder of the Black Consciousness Movement in South Africa. He was detained by security police and tortured to death in 1977. He could have preached hate and division and people would have followed him— there were enough grounds to do so—but he didn't.

Generative leadership comes from the basic orientation out of which we live and act

[Doug]   Whatever the Apartheid state did to him, he stood above all for a powerful, all-encompassing end that he called "true humanity."

STEVE BIKO'S "QUEST FOR TRUE HUMANITY"

Raised in a poor Xhosa family, Bantu Stephen Biko (1946–1977) grew up in the Eastern Cape, South Africa, and later studied medicine at the University of Natal. He was a leading figure in the Black Consciousness Movement during the late 1960s and 1970s but opposed anti-white racism.

The government saw Biko as a serious subversive threat and placed him under a banning order in 1973, severely restricting his activities. He remained politically active but was arrested in August 1977. Severely beaten in detention by state security police, Biko died from brain injuries. Though the state tried to prevent it, over 20,000 people attended his funeral. Many songs and works of art and a film, *Cry Freedom*, celebrate his legacy.

Biko stood, above all, for a powerful, all-encompassing, and inclusive end. He wrote[2]: "The racism we meet does not only exist on an individual basis: it is also institutionalized to make it look like the South African way of life. Although of late there has been a feeble attempt to gloss over the overt racist elements in the system, it is still true that the system derives its nourishment from the existence of anti-black attitudes in society.

Ours [African] is a true man-centred [sic] society whose sacred tradition is that of sharing. We must reject … the individualistic cold approach to life that is the cornerstone of the Anglo-Boer culture. We must seek to restore to the black man the great importance we used to give to human relations, the high regard for people and their property and for life in general, to reduce the triumph of technology over man and the materialistic element that is slowly creeping into our society …

Racism does not only imply exclusion of one race by another—it always presupposes that the exclusion is for the purposes of subjugation. Blacks have had enough experience as objects of racism not to wish to turn the tables. While it may be relevant now to talk about black in relation to white, we must not make this our preoccupation, for it can be a negative exercise. As we proceed further towards the achievements of our goals let us talk more about ourselves and our struggle and less about whites.

We have set out on a quest for true humanity, and somewhere on the distant horizon we can see the glittering prize. Let us march forth with courage and determination, drawing strength from our common plight and our brotherhood [sic]. In time we shall be in a position to bestow upon South Africa the greatest gift possible—a more human face."

[Jim]   Biko looked beyond his own interests—even the interests of his own movement. The "end" of his leadership was not a narrow one at all. Because he made that intention, that end, so clear, he was deeply respected. His charisma helped but it's what he stood for, with such integrity, that made all the difference.

[Doug]   I want to add something very important, though. *You don't have to be a hero* to live with the same kind of intention! It's a capacity we *all* have as human beings, no matter who we are.

[Jim]   That is crucial. It's no coincidence that Biko inspired everyone then but his generative message resounds today, still speaking to the highest and best of which we are capable. Here's a similar thought from Nobel Peace Prize winner Desmond Tutu expressing something central to generative leadership."

There is something in us that refuses to be regarded as less than human. We are created for freedom.

[Doug]   Ah, yes, you are linking the idea of freedom to what you mean by generative leadership! "Created for freedom," a great phrase!

[Jim]   We need to be very careful about what kind of freedom this is, though. It can't be merely freedom of choice or opportunity, the kind of freedom that advertising or marketing celebrates.

[Doug]   Mmm, for me it's something very different. I think of it this way: We can be liberated from oppression and still act or live in ways that simply reflect a new self-interest. To be free from something still doesn't tell us what we think freedom is *for*.

[Jim]   Ah, that brings us back to Biko's "quest for true humanity." The key question, of course, is what does "true humanity" mean in thinking about our freedom? Here are some thoughts on what's at its core—take a look:

1. *We are creatures of nature*. We share much with other living beings, and we must respect that. We are also limited by what's possible in nature, both in ourselves and in what lies outside of us (think of how climate change is affecting everything).
2. But, crucially, *we are not determined by nature: we can change or transform it!* In this sense, we have freedom over nature.
3. We do this through *extra*-ordinary capacities we have (*to a degree* true of no other creature we know) that enable us to *see, and bring into being, new possibilities* and potentials that nature itself cannot create.
4. These capacities allow us to enter into and act in the world not just through instinct but *intentionally*—towards ends we determine.
5. We can choose to become independent of nature through technology, or interdependent with it through creative interaction. We also continually create new ways of *organizing how we live* together in our family, community, or society.
6. All of this, which every one of us possesses, is our **creative freedom**.

[Doug]   That's potent. I need to think about it. But why do you say our capacity to "see new possibilities and potentials" in nature and bring them into being is "extra-ordinary"?

[Jim]   Well, many animals, birds, fish, even insects, can also do amazing things, and we learn more about that every day. We surely aren't the only sentient or intelligent creatures on earth.

[Doug]   Yet clearly they don't come close to what humans can do.

[Jim]   No, and that *difference* makes all the difference! Even something as simple as controlling fire to cook food or make iron is extraordinary, never mind inventing the hoe or plough, building chairs and tables, harnessing electricity, launching aeroplanes into the sky carrying hundreds of people, computers, genetic engineering …

[Doug]   Yup. Nature, and other creatures, don't and can't do any of that intentionally. We can and do. This powerful capacity to *change* nature tells us something crucial about ourselves—not least about the *massive responsibility* we carry for what we are capable of.

[Jim]   That's the crunch. It's really worth summarizing this, so here are the key points …

The capacities we have allow us to … initiate sequences of events that change nature in ways it could never do on its own, and shape and change the way we behave or live together, and this is our creative freedom.

This creative freedom is inherent. We are born with it by virtue of being human, so it can't be taken away from us (except by killing us).

Creative freedom is totally democratic: no person is without it as long as they are recognizably human. Even in the most limiting circumstances (being a quadriplegic, or in solitary confinement, even under torture to some extent) every person can exercise it.

Our capacities are a gift. We don't choose them, and we didn't give them to ourselves. Good in themselves, we can use them one way or another.

What we do with our creative freedom is up to us. We can, and do, decide to act towards particular ends that, ultimately, no one else chooses for us. Someone else may tell us what to do and how to be, but we still have to decide for ourselves—any and every time we exercise our creative freedom in the world.

It's also potentially very dangerous, for we can use it for destructive ends too. So powerful is it that we can, through choice or neglect, destroy the world itself and ourselves along with it.

Nothing forces us to use it for one end or another; we have to choose which. That's what it means to speak of our moral responsibility as human beings.

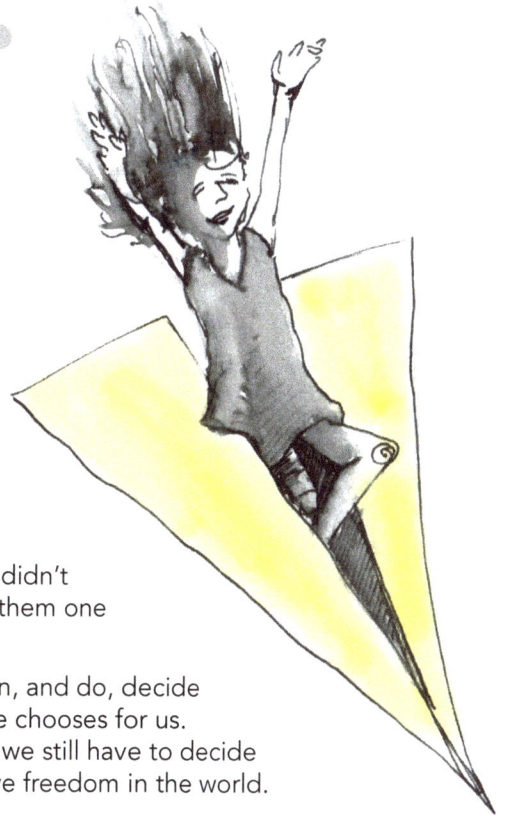

[Jim]   So we see why and how freedom is connected to generative leadership, and why it has to do with the ends we pursue. Acting for "limited" ends like mere self-interest couldn't be generative. But when someone lives out of the best and highest ends we are capable of as human beings we respect them deeply. Actually, what we respect, *because we are no less human*, is something we are also capable of—with vision, courage and the will.

[Doug]   And we aren't talking about what great and famous figures do. We all possess this creative freedom and can take responsibility for it in generative ways!

TWO LETTERS

Dear Liz,

I hope that you're well and enjoying your time in Brazil. Doug M and I had an interesting discussion on generative leadership while walking in Newlands Forest, and I thought that I'd share some of our thoughts with you as you are working on this topic for your Master's Degree. And in the hope that you could respond with your own reflections.

In our discussion, we recognized the fact that even though we are relational creatures, we are slow developers and need the care of others over a long time as we mature and that much of what we need to learn comes from others, past and present, from the moment we are aware and throughout our lives.

However, we also agreed that we are capable of "seeing" new possibilities or potentials in our world and are able to transform them through the symbolic systems that we acquire and develop—like languages or mathematics or rituals. In the process of inventing these *symbolic systems*, we generate concepts, ideas, or theories we can put into practice.

As we walked through the forest and looked at the trees around us, we both remembered various things we had made from wood over the years; shelves, chairs, tables, even a boat. We commented on the fact that *none* of those things were in the trees except as *possibilities*! In that moment we looked at a tall pine and said; "that would make a great table!" We had both generated the table as a concept and in a split second connected it with other concepts—a saw, a hammer and chisel, a design.

We could see that the symbolic systems we had developed helped us see new possibilities upon which we could act and that this is a skill which gives us huge advantages that other creatures simply don't have—though, to be fair, they have other skills—who wouldn't like to fly? We then laughed and said that we'd probably be extinct without these capacities, we just aren't that good at other ways of surviving!

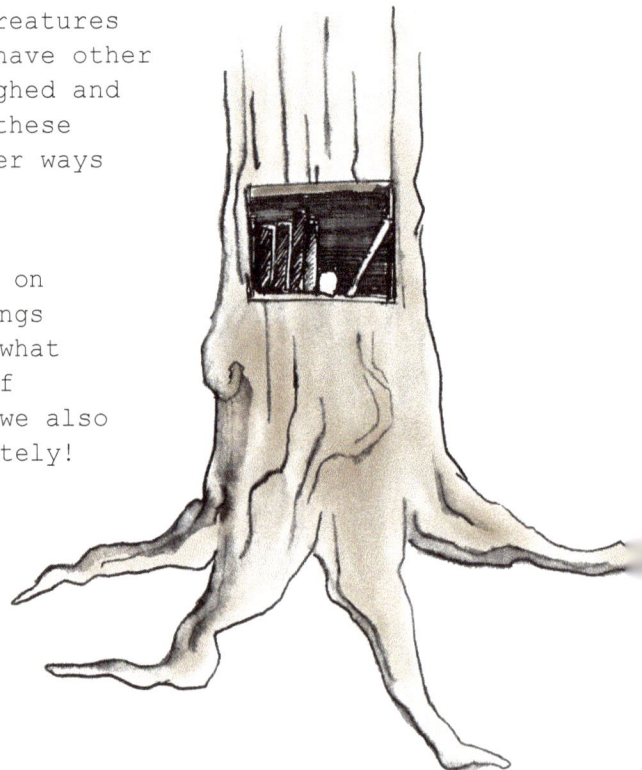

As we walked, Doug felt that, as part of our discussion, this tree example focused merely on the technical, pragmatic, or theoretical things we can do and have to learn and that it somewhat represented limited "ends"—a mere "culture of skills". He said that it was important that we also have to learn *why* any of this matters ultimately! That the questions 'for what purpose?', 'for whose good?', 'towards what ends do we do anything at all?', 'how ought we to live?', would direct us towards "*cultivating our will*."

Let me end there. Looking forward to your thoughts.

Jim

Dear Jim (and Doug)

What a stimulating letter! My first thoughts are about our moral responsibility to nature, to ourselves, and with our creative freedom. As humans we depend heavily upon others to help us understand what it means to assume moral responsibility for our creative freedom.

Like you, I lament the fact that for many people skills are often seen as the most important thing, and that only that which can be measured or counted or seen is regarded as really real and that we too easily set aside what we *can't see*.

You say that if our creative freedom is to be generative it can't be merely for some narrow need or self-interest—our own, or our group's or our institution, culture, tradition or whomever's self-interest.

What strikes me is that there's a kind of imperative here, a kind of command—not from somewhere else but from *inside ourselves*, about how we choose to live and what we intend with our action, about what ends really govern us.

I guess, this lies at the heart of what we call human dignity, and it's what Immanuel Kant meant when he said that we should never treat persons, including ourselves, as mere means to some other end but always as an end in themselves. It is here that our family, community, religious or political leaders, or any other authority, can also help us develop and apply our capacities of creative freedom.

For me, what is clear is that *we must make the decision* about what we will follow and what not. We, not someone else, must decide to what ends we will ultimately act and why. That makes us responsible for it and it allows us to hold others responsible for what they do. In this way it makes it a moral responsibility for the whole, for more than one's own organization or group. It helps each of us use our own agency by enhancing, supporting and sustaining our capacities of the creative freedom you often speak about.

> *There's a kind of imperative, a kind of command—not from somewhere else but from inside ourselves—about how we choose to live and what we intend*

So, yes! Creative freedom requires that the *ends* towards which we lead are as important as the means we use, not as a socially expedient imperative but as something we must do to be fully human. They transcend the limits of any particular interest or group for the sake of all and the sake of the whole.

Let me "end" there though I feel we are just beginning.

Warmly

Liz

SOCIAL FORMS OF LEADERSHIP

Some speak of leadership but only mean the practices and behaviours that promise things called "results" – "managements by results" is a popular paradigm. Sometimes they speak of "outcomes" but only mean the things that happen shortly after the acts of those called leaders. We would like to distance ourselves from such instrumental notions. People drawn into the learning networks of the Barefoot Collective, the Leading Causes of Life Initiative, Stakeholder Health, and 100 Million Lives want more, usually because we have all drunk of that thin gruel and found it too weak to sustain the journey that matters most. We crave the experience of being part of great work because it calls us to great things, not just because of someone called a leader (even if sometimes we find ourselves in that role).

We crave the experience of being part of great work because it calls us to great things, not just because of someone called a leader

However, we may still be tempted by other lesser ideas—especially that of the heroic leader! In our networks, we may decry the mere accumulation of wealth or power, but we might also like to accumulate a reputation for suffering, or the eloquence of lament, perhaps to be the bard of justice. When we grow beyond such entertainments and distractions, we are left with the real question about how we might give our lives purposefully to the things that matter more than ourselves. That doesn't stop us living ourselves. The learning networks that nurture this book are often marked by laughter, delight and a sense of vitality.

Life nurtures us even as we give ourselves to its ways. Life generates life, leaving us with more of it than we expected. Generative leadership is not a trick technique and it does not deplete us. Even when we are drawn closer to suffering, we are not left just in sadness, but want to respond in a creative, life-affirming way. This is so surprising that it begs for a better vocabulary than "work" or "labour."

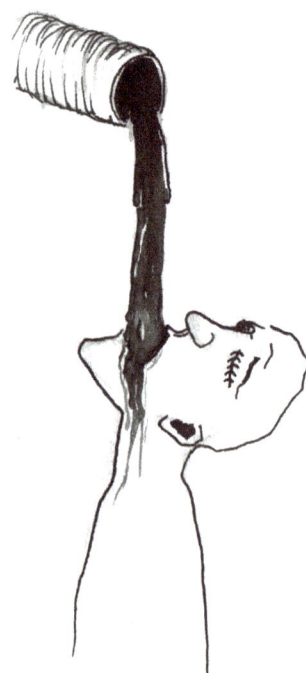

The word that comes closest is found in Greek, *poiesis*. It's from the root of 'to make', the same root from which we get 'poetry.' Poiesis describes the actions that transform and continue the life of the world. It's not just about technical labours, or simply making something, any more than a poem is about putting words into a technically correct order. Poetry—and poiesis—is not about the work at all, but about the ends that transform labour into something that is life-giving or generative. Poiesis merges thought with matter and time, that links person with the world, that 'calls forth a new world.'

It's the kind of work that leadership facilitates among those with whom they share generative labour. It is in this kind of leadership in which the ones called "leaders" lose themselves and then find themselves again as one of a shared community. The verb "lead" no longer describes the actions of one person or even a group of people with official roles, but an ensemble who, together, participate in calling forth at least a bit of a new world.

Sometimes this happens. Most of the time the work of calling forth a new world is, well, let's speak frankly, a pain in the ass.

Any group of humans—*especially* those with urgent love for the melting planet—work as a ragged gaggle, with grinding friction and unpredictable distraction. We do not wish to romanticize the work of life, this poiesis. Many parts of what needs to happen are accomplished with other social forms, all participatory, all as honourable as a well-crafted shovel used with purpose and energy. Everything does look like high art.

At one of the gatherings of some of the authors of this book in Greyton, South Africa, not all of our work was crafting language; we had to eat, too. Some like Beulah were exquisite in the high arts of the kitchen, blending ingredients into satisfying meals; others such as Gary were better at cleaning up. It is said that during a tour of the Kennedy Space Launch Center a janitor was asked what she did. "I'm putting a man on the moon," she proudly responded. And she was correct.

The art of leadership is the facility of sensing what kind of generative work needs what kind of generative form during its different phases of emergence. Some of it is a great deal like work of any kind, even tedious in part. And some is nearly mystical. Just a couple of hills over from where Gary cleaned the grease off the lunch pots, he watched as the full moon crested the high ridge above, breaking through the ragged shards of a clearing storm. A moment of poiesis. Generative leadership honors every stage of every participating soul, every craft and gift.

Generative leadership honors every stage of every participating soul, every craft and gift

So … what does one … do … with all these possibilities? What does this work actually look like in practice?

The work of life takes many social forms, but it helps to see that there are four very basic categories which may include everyone in a group in different ways at different times. Let us imagine that what the world needs is a book written in a participatory manner suited to the subject of, say, generative leadership. There are many components of this discrete goal (itself part of a grand intention for the life of the whole world). Let us assume that the group of authors needs to meet, imagining it easier or at least more appropriate to write together. You can see all four basic social forms in action.

The work of life takes many social forms

1. There are projects to be done, ideally voluntarily. Somebody needs to cook, which seems right for a form called **a committee**. This is a set of activities with known methods and resources that can be best accomplished in a group that knows how to do these things.

2. Frequently a committee that has agreed on what to do delegates **projects**. So after the meal the committee has cooked and then eaten, the dishes must be cleaned. This is a project best delegated to one or two people (all that fits around the sink). A project is something that somebody knows how to do and they do it and it is then done. If it is not done well, the group may become sick quite quickly and there will be no book.

3. A book is a lot more complicated, especially if done together by a group of creative and diverse humans. This is beyond a committee, which can only accomplish things with known and agreed tools and criteria. A book needs a group of people to organize itself around a hope that is not defined in advance, to be accomplished in a manner that must emerge out of the group without entirely knowing how or what that means. A book done by a group of authors emerges from a collaboration that is limited in space and time. It is a place—a domain—that is limited to the purposes that attract and hold the members of the group for as long as they choose. The key to a **limited domain collaboration** (LDC) is the limits. Inherently unknowable in detail and method, but with a perimeter agreed on that contains the energy. Sometimes the limited domain may grow (another book! Or: Let's hold a meeting, too! Or: Let's try this on another subject!). And sometimes it shrinks. Sometimes the group never wants to see each other again. The genius of the LDC is that they don't have to.

4. Sometimes the book is just the seed of something even more unpredictable, ambiguous and open ended. Every great movement can trace its seminal moment to the convergence of people who find themselves part of something more powerful and transformational. We call this social form **Poiesis**. The point is that all these social forms are part of the work of life, all necessary but only in the context of giving life a chance. It is leadership to discern which of the forms is best at which phase.

So in any given challenge, generative agents need to work with and be skilled in all four basic generative social forms: *projects, committees, limited domain collaboration and poiesis*. The first two—projects and committees—are familiar to you if you've made it through kindergarten and into institutional life. The third, "limited domain collaboration," is a more complex and open level of collaboration. Poiesis is a sustained, highly generative relationship that you've probably experienced without having language to describe it as we have.

All of social forms serve life and all of them have both social and technical characteristics that allow them to serve life better. This framing is not intended to create a hierarchy of value or life-ness; just a differentiation in function. All of these forms/ frames are crucial, but particularly those at either end—project and Poiesis—influence the whole continuum.

All social forms ought to serve life, and all have communicative and technical aspects that can help serve life better

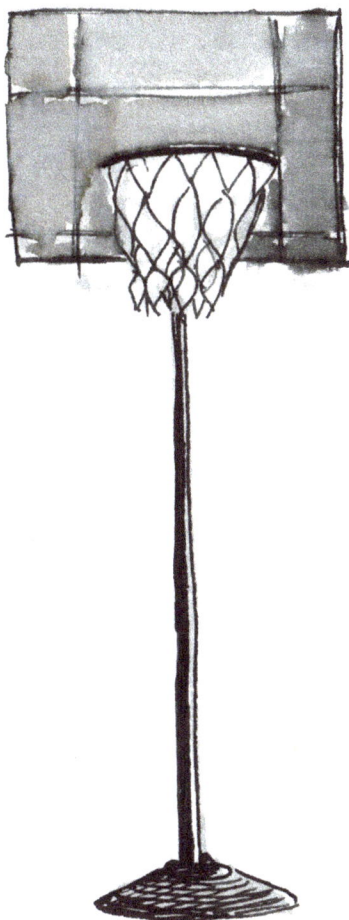

The social forms have different strengths that make them fit different kinds of necessary work. It may be less obvious that each of them also has inherent weaknesses that can be dangerous, if overlooked.

A project can lose sight of the overall goal. It can be instrumental, not generative. It can invade the overall process dumbing down complexity in a way that is distracting and wasteful. A committee can use its power to offload risk or it can lend its credibility to avoiding risk through doing as little as possible. A Limited Domain Collaboration can get the limits wrong. Going too broad too fast may discourage meaningful collaboration. Going too narrow and too slow makes the process not worth the time. The energy dissipates before it flows. Poiesis work can devolve into a club or support group instead of generating action for the world.

Generative leadership helps social movements move and not get stuck. The key is to keep all the countless components held in the light of the generative goals on the horizon that draw us beyond ourselves. In this sense every part of the movement resonates with some of the energy of poiesis as every bit of it is needed to make the world. The linking logic is fluid, dynamic, fuelled by meaning and hope, not fear. These are all characteristics of poiesis, which suggests that leadership itself is more like poetry, helping humans find their right relationship to each other around what is essential and less like the technical assembly of discrete parts.

It is as easy to underestimate generative strength as it is to overestimate the power of technical processes as projects and committees. Generative phenomena look subtle and slow compared to the dumb blunt weight of technical force and money. They can end, but not give life; steal, but not create; crush, but not raise. Life literally goes on without them, sometime without them even noticing. This is most true in the purest form of generative structure, poiesis.

> *Leadership is more like poetry, helping humans find right relationship to each other*

Poiesis has the least formal structure and a casual attitude about concrete goals. Almost pure generativity, it has strong but foggy governance and operates outside the normal organizational calendar and sense of budget. Those involved tend to laugh more than seems entirely appropriate. It makes up words and conceptual tools, which give it curious liberty to see the world in a manner distinctively free from obligation to existing guilds or control.

Because of its raw creative potential, it can influence and steer entire fields, even invent one. This also gives poiesis a dangerous quality that can turn inward and tribal, serving the worst possible social and political instincts. The untethered nature of poiesis is tested by one question, that of its ends; is it generative for the whole world?

Most of the important learnings in life occur in social structures with strong qualities of poiesis. A poiesis forms a bit like a hurricane, spinning off a social or conceptual desert in an undervalued bleak place, such as Africa or Memphis, and always works as predictably as a metronome.

> *'Life is what happens while you are busy making other plans'*
> — John Lennon

Built for generosity, generation, generativity, poiesis does the hardest possible lift in social and political relationships—it changes mind, strengthens heart, finds the seed of courage and encourages valour

It spins in social space and emerges in what happens in between a handful, then more, people—usually edge kinds themselves, even if working in legitimate institutions. Those individuals have strong enough egos to do what they want, but for some reason—perhaps their mothers, as in some cases—have a strong inclination to want to do things that are good for others, especially those different from their mother tongue and tribe.

Much of what we learned about the social patterns of boundary leaders applies to those drawn to poiesis. We learned a better language for the relationships that emerge and are sustained for decades by boundary leaders: webs of trust, webs of transformation. These webs are not weak, they are gossamer threads of steel without the vulnerability of rigid, canalized leadership.

Built for generosity, generation, generativity, poiesis does the hardest possible lift in social and political relationships—it changes mind, strengthens heart, finds the seed of courage and encourages valour. It finds a way, like life.

How could we ever know; but we suspect that the early small nomadic groups finding their way out of Africa, across the Aleutians, into Patagonia and New Zealand and the furthest reaches of what is now Scandinavia had the capacity to do so because of the huge advantage poiesis gives in a journey of radical uncertainty.

Generosity, not suspicion, generation not just acquisition; generativity linked to expansiveness, not just violence. There were plenty of other more violent bipeds. Maybe humans found a way because this little evolutionary offering had the advantage of poiesis. It would explain a lot. Such a hypothesis is classic poiesis all by itself.

EMERGING FORMS OF SOCIAL CHANGE LEADERSHIP AND ORGANIZATION

Doug R's Story

The struggle against Apartheid in the 1980s was life defining for me as a young activist. In our successes and failures of mobilizing and organizing I discovered a love for organization development, social process design and facilitation. This has been at the heart of my vocation since, working as an organization development practitioner across Africa and occasionally beyond, supporting the development of organizational culture, strategy, practice, leadership and learning for a range of civil society organisations and social movements. It's been quite a ride, so much more of an education in the ways of human evolution and transformation than I ever bargained for.

And so I have used this writing opportunity to explore what I have witnessed of the evolution of civil society organisations and leadership over the years and what I have learned about the deeper and most vital struggle we have, way beyond Apartheid, to become more fully human.

The struggle in South Africa in the 1980s consumed us in processes of mobilizing, educating, protesting and witnessing the unfolding of the unstoppable will of millions of citizens inside South Africa and across the globe, rallying to toss out the white regime and overturn its awful system.

What kind of organization and leadership held us together through those tempestuous years? Leadership was essentially *vanguardist*: small, tight-knit groups of politically assertive leaders, under orders from the movement in exile, mobilized and held us together through a series of campaigns and smaller actions aimed at putting pressure on the state on as many fronts as possible. On the surface our organisations were quite flat and the campaign meetings had a vein of democracy as we engaged in healthy ideological, strategic and tactical debates and made democratic decisions.

> *We seldom questioned decisions handed down when the divide between right and wrong was clear with little to argue about*

But the key direction, the governing ideology and the way we were organized and deployed, was largely set from above, with all playing a disciplined role. The big decisions were made behind the scenes in secret caucuses, something most of us knew and accepted given that police spies were known to have infiltrated many organisations. Our leaders, the higher they got, were classically heroic, with Nelson Mandela and Oliver Tambo being the icons. We seldom questioned decisions handed down when the divide between right and wrong was clear with little to argue about. We had to be "disciplined" so as not to confuse or play into the hands of provocateurs sent into our ranks to divide us.

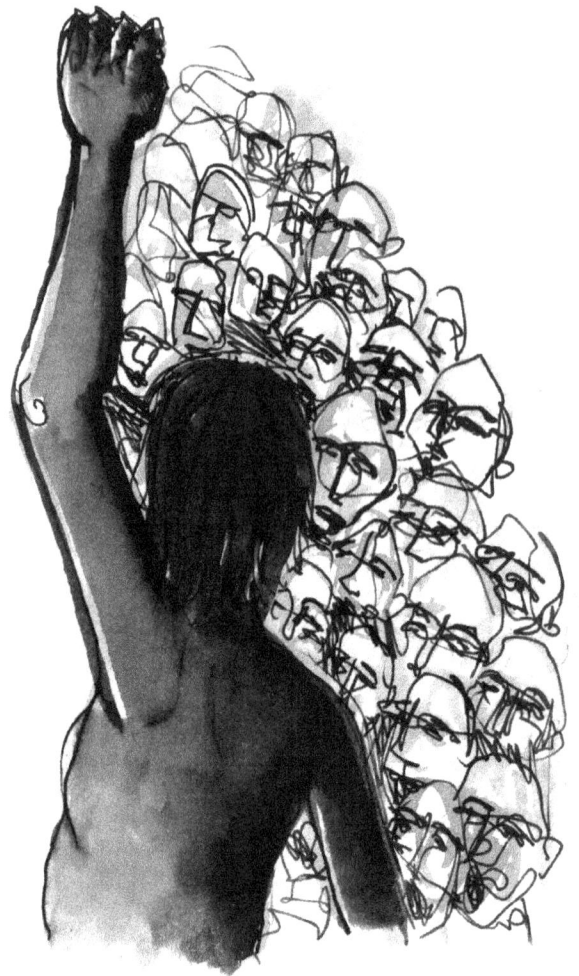

The struggle was unambiguous, black and white. We were part of a long series of generations who had been well trained to respect and even fear authority, and could be easily mobilized and organized. We listened and we followed orders. Fast forward today, to the individualized millennial age of social media, with seemingly leaderless movements of young people with multiple, intersecting causes, easy to mobilize but often impossible to organize in familiar ways! More of that later.

In the struggle against Apartheid, with a clear goal and a more predictable context than today, where it was much easier to anticipate what the government would do, we worked within hierarchical forms of organization with some space for local democracy, innovation and adaptation.

THE POST-APARTHEID EVOLUTION OF CIVIL SOCIETY ORGANISATIONS

In post-Apartheid South Africa, the context is more complex, unpredictable, and rapidly changing. Forms of organization have become far more varied and adaptive. As social change activism and forms of organization and leadership have themselves changed, I have witnessed several competing thrusts, described below.

A. The growing professionalisation of activism

There has been a growing professionalization of activism organized within the NGO sector over the last two decades, mostly under donor pressure, with two diverging trends:

Corporatising NGOs

The first trend has seen the development of NGOs as corporate entities, closely resembling the business world, following so-called "best practice models" with business plans, corporate branding, and performance management systems etc., and little evidence of the kind of generative leadership we have been exploring. Donors no longer fund organisations themselves but put out tenders for projects for which NGOs must compete, while also being encouraged, or even coerced, to collaborate with each other. Many of these structures, learning from corporates to stay lean and mean, have become project managing organisations, sub-contracting work to a growing legion of contract workers or freelancers. Indeed, the large international accounting firms have now entered this market, competing for the same work and using the same contract workers.

Internally, many if not most of these corporatizing NGOs are beset by overwork, stress and burnout, with strong hierarchies and bullying, pushed by donors (mostly international and government) who have little imagination or understanding of how the world of social change works and who ask for results that are difficult to achieve or to account for.

These donors are often themselves subject to similar pressures from their back-donors, usually governments who prioritize programmes according to their own foreign policy objectives. The compliance systems, built around business-like projects plans, serve to manage mistrust between partners rather than to mobilize trust in generative ways.

Although it's difficult to make too many sweeping judgements, I can say that, of the hundreds of large NGOs that I and my colleagues have worked with over the years, few are achieving the kind of sustainable society-changing results that they have promised and planned, and some, rather than helping, may well have served to tame and soften the anger rising from the growing masses of the marginalized and impoverished in the country.

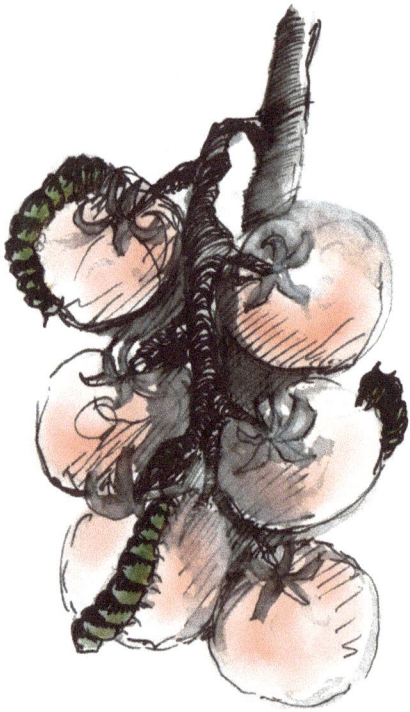

Compliance systems serve to manage mistrust rather than build trust between partners

Alliances of smaller NGOs

Those NGOs that do have an impact tend to be the smaller ones, being more values-driven, agile and adaptable, less reliant on delivering resources and more on unlocking local resourcefulness, as well as being friendlier and more humane places to work, bringing the best in their staff and volunteers. Unfortunately, they tend to lack the marketing and PR capacity to attract good funding and many have closed over the years or had their staff poached by the larger NGOs.

The ones that are surviving and making a difference tend to be those who are able to work more collaboratively and creatively in alliances, supported by smaller international donors, some of whom have connected their work directly to supporting social movements (as described below). Organizationally, you will find a variety of adaptive management forms that enable them to learn their way through the many challenges they face. They tend not to have to compete for funding but have built longer-term relationships with the smaller donors who have a greater understanding and willingness to learn about what the real work of social change is.

If you are looking for good examples of generative leaders, working from and guided by developmental and empowering values and principles, you are more likely to find them here.

B. Post-modern grassroots activism

Another organizing thrust can be found in a new generation of Millennials who have moved into grassroots activism in student or community movements. But how different things are today from the struggles of the 20th century! Most activists emerging over these past two decades have had little of the kind of experience of struggle we had in the 1980s.

The younger activists I see today have an individual and creative freedom of spirit that we simply could not have in the struggle of the 1980s. They may be more conscious and more easily mobilized (both through social media) but are not so easy to organize in conventional ways. Some of the work we have been called to do is to help resolve conflicts that arise from this tension between post-modern consciousness and modern organizational forms—there is little patience for older forms of disciplined organization. But there is some interesting experimentation with new organizational and leadership forms emerging in the playing out of this tension.

Let me re-emphasize: *leaders* are only one form of *leadership*. Many observers have remarked on how leaderless and disorganized the new political movements seem to be at times, but these observers have not made this distinction. These movements are not *leadershipless* and the organizational forms they use do not follow recognizable hierarchies and straight lines for executing decisions.

Leaders' are only one form of leadership

A new generation of Millennials have moved into grassroots activism

In fact, their leadership often appears to be fluid, more located in the processes and outcomes of smaller and larger forums where direction is heavily debated by people with a wide range of interests, often from a variety of contexts. They experiment with many kinds of self-organizing forms, heavily reliant on social media, using complex ways of networking and communication that are not always visible to outsiders. Prominent examples would be the mass mobilizations of the Arab Spring, the Occupy Movement in the USA, the student protests in Chile and South Africa etc.

There is some resonance with the kinds of facilitative, generative leadership we describe in this Barefoot Guide, but there are also important differences and some key challenges. Mainly, although these new forms can gather great steam, mobilize large numbers of people, and at the best of times, force society to look again and maybe respond, they also suffer from burn-out, a lack of momentum, and difficulty in defining not so much what they want but how change can happen. Demands are often framed as things the government must get right so that if the battle is won and the government concedes the ball is put back in their bureaucratic court. Then the movement dissipates, thinking it has won only to discover that if the promised demands do get addressed by a government department it usually misinterprets or subverts the original intention.

C. Social movement activism

The third thrust is found in many current social movements, like Via Campesina and Shack Dwellers International. It brings together the best qualities and elements of two dimensions: contemporary activism that focuses on mobilizing, and then professional adaptive management, which focuses on sustainable *organizing*.

Each of these processes is central to the challenges of contemporary social leadership, actually for generative leadership.

Mobilizing in this context is less about leaders trying to move things and more about unlocking latent energies, freeing up the will of people to act. The roots of this will lie in the past, the present or the future.

From past injustices comes the will for redress, for compensation, for restoration of rights, even humanity, lost or denied. From the present comes the will for righting current injustices, inequalities or inhuman conditions. From future visions comes the will born of hope and faith that things can be better. From all three comes the will for acting collectively, the unlocking of social power. What is being mobilized is often a dynamic mix of anger, frustration, hope and solidarity.

What is being mobilized is often a dynamic mix of anger, frustration, hope and solidarity

Organizing in this context is about facilitating the processes through which human energies are brought together towards achieving common aims in ways that are *manageable and sustainable*, so that they do not suffer from the kind of burnout described in the second thrust above. It's definitely not about the controlling mechanisms of vanguardism described in the first thrust that work less and less in our post-modern age. Instead, key is enabling *self-control*, with local initiative, under agreed values and towards agreed aims.

Interestingly, many social movements, while being understandably cautious, even suspicious of the kind of corporatizing NGOs described above, work in strong alliances with a few small NGOs, who provide financial, research or development services for them.

Several practices are common to organisations like Via Campesina and Shack Dwellers International that encapsulate leadership in the processes of mobilizing and organizing. Various horizontal learning rituals, like exchange visits, connecting fellow farmers, neighbours, or co-workers in ways that grow resilient relationships.

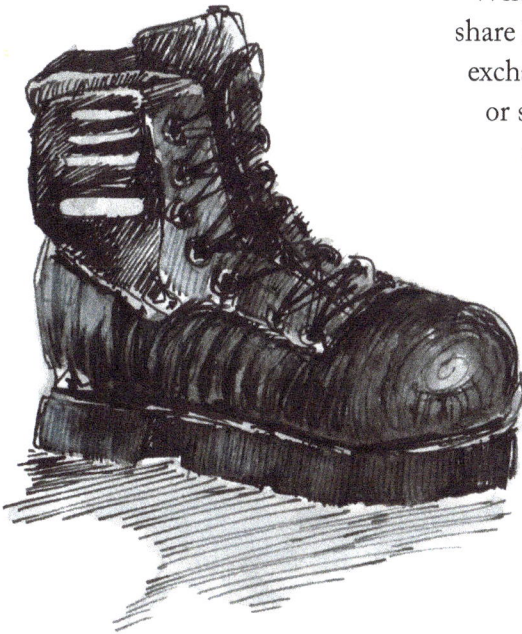

When farmers are encouraged to visit other farmers to share lessons and innovations, not only is valuable knowledge exchanged but trusting relationships of solidarity are created or strengthened, laying foundations for future collective action. This is leadership in process. When women living as neighbours in poor communities are mobilized to form daily savings groups, they elect one of their own to collect (they are called collectors) and bank their money, thus identifying the women that they trust the most. These collectors, as proto-leaders, identified from being trusted, are then given further opportunities to develop their leadership capabilities.

This quality of being trusted (because you are trustworthy) may be the most vital for the generative leadership we describe in this Guide. Had the women's groups each held an election to elect a leader rather than a collector, based on their idea of what a leader should look and sound like, it is quite likely that people would be elected who can speak well, who can project confidence, but who are less trustworthy and less likely to authentically represent their community. Confidence and public speaking can be taught, but trustworthiness has to have already been learned.

This example of how good potential leaders can be identified and nurtured highlights the challenge for society in all its organisations and institutions. Why do we continue to elect or appoint the wrong people into leadership positions and how might we do this differently? How do we change the narrative of what leaders should do and indeed what leadership is?

Implications for leadership

From this broad scan of the development of leadership and organization in civil society there are, for me, several implications for the nature of the kind of leaders (and leadership) required:

- They pay strong attention to the kind of common values and purpose that can help to guide and direct self-driven members working in collective efforts. Practically, this may mean facilitating conversations that help members to surface and deepen the values and aims that matter to them, as their own, and then to commit to them;
- They are always on the lookout for what is blocking or hindering positive energies and for where positive energy is flowing. Practically, this means being interested in and knowing what people want, not as defensive or fearful responses, but as generative, generous human beings;
- They seek to facilitate rather than control the processes of sense-making and decision-making by members. Practically, this means knowing how to ask questions that help people to think for themselves, in conversation with each other, and through that, to co-create new knowledge and ideas to take the process forward;

Know how to ask questions that help people to think for themselves, in conversation with each other

- They look for ways to enable more self-organisation and responsibility, supporting others to take on their own leadership. Less control and more self-control. Practically, this means finding the right balance between challenging people to *take* responsibility (it is not enough to give it) and supporting them through their fears and self-doubts;
- They have faith in the outcomes of messy, unpredictable processes that are guided by good values and aims, where the way forward is to navigate the complexities of life through learning from experience and creative experimenting, without falling back on command and control behaviours and conventional certainties.

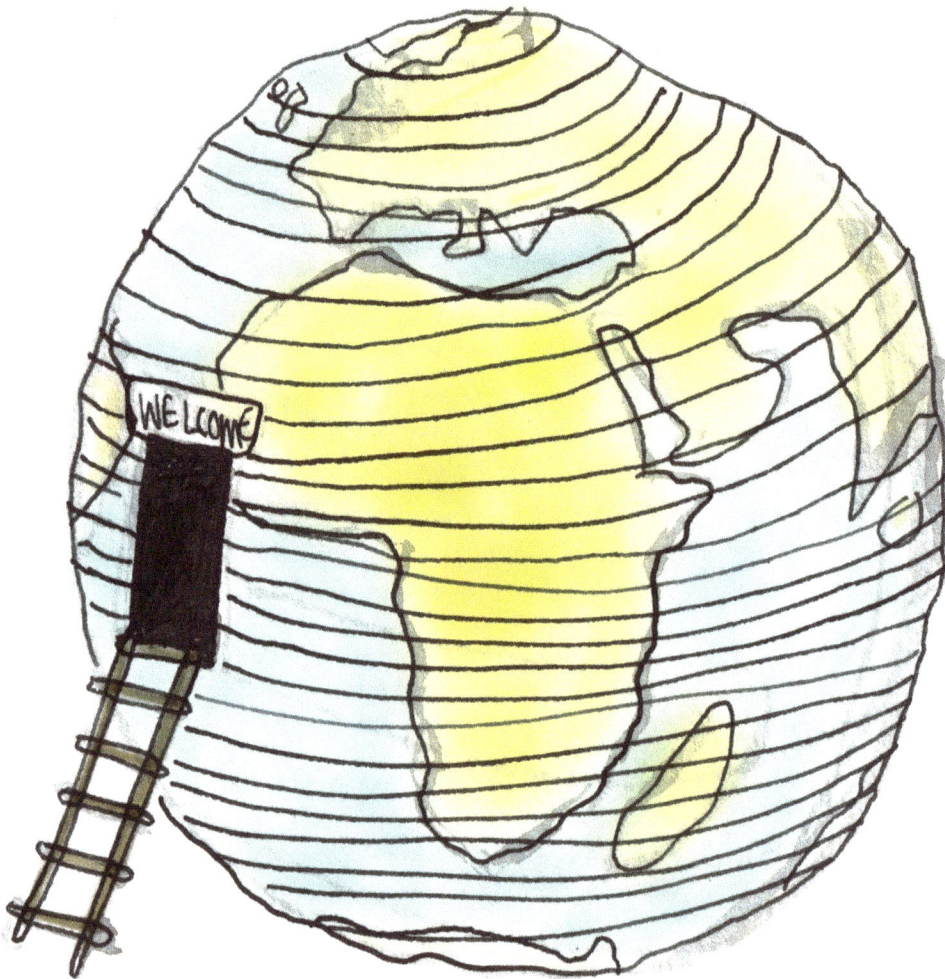

CHAPTER 4

WORKING INSIDE THE RIVER
Practicing Leadership within the Turbulence

So far we have described the kind of leadership we have inherited from the past, embedded in the canalized command and control nature and cultures of the living systems in which we live on earth today. We have described the challenges this has left us with, but we have also presented a different, contrasting vision of what life requires and what kind of leadership can be generative of life. Now we look further into the mindsets and practices of generative leadership through cycles of observing and understanding life to designing responses and initiatives to acting.

The image of working inside a river, as we move into a turbulent future, dramatically mirrors the reality of leadership processes that do not just 'go with the flow' but have conscious purpose and agency. Not all leadership is conscious but generative leadership is, in choosing to enter the river to engage the turbulence, to go to where the flows and forces of change exist. Purpose is found within the truth of the work itself, not in this or that result. That's because life in its fullness is itself the purpose.

Generative leadership doesn't try to bring life for others to take but looks for it wherever it grows, connects to it, helps unlock it if need be, to find its best, human expression

This chapter is about entering the river, about seeing, experiencing and engaging it from the inside, consciously, humanely and respectfully. Generative leadership does not try to bring life for others to take but looks for it wherever it grows, connecting its own life with it, helping unlock it if need be, to find its best, human expression.

DRAGONS CAN BE BEATEN
Using stories to explore and understand an organization in crisis

"Fairy tales are more than true; not because they tell us that dragons exist, but because they tell us that dragons can be beaten."

– Neil Gaiman, "Coraline" –

A few years ago, I was working in an organization that found itself in the midst of a crisis. As colleagues, we were struggling to communicate effectively with each other, with staff burnout, a shortage of funds to support teaching faculties and projects, a general lack of motivation and no clear engagement and direction from the leaders of the organization. With the help of a facilitator, we were led through a process of 'surfacing' our issues by creating folk tales to characterize our crisis situation. Here are four of the stories that emerged.

A facilitator helped lead us through a process of 'surfacing' our issues by creating folk tales to characterize our crisis situation

'There was once an orphan child, who was left in the forest to fend for herself. She was alone and cold, her once beautiful garment dirty and tattered, and she did not have a morsel of food to sustain her. As she looked around, all she could see was the forest of trees ...'

'A young man went off to seek his fortune. He came to a great ocean and saw a large ship with bright sails. He asked to work on the ship in exchange for food and passage. Soon the ship left the harbour and the young man worked on the deck scrubbing the wooden floors. However, a storm arose, and the ship was buffeted against the winds and tossed about in the wild waves. The sailors worked hard to steady the sails, but the young man soon realized that there was no captain on board ...'

'There was an old woman who had many children. Even though she loved them dearly, she could not feed and clothe them fully. She went out to work in the fields every day, but at nightfall she returned with a basket filled only with a few wrinkled carrots, small potatoes and limp spinach leaves. The ragged children were sent off to bed with rumbling tummies ...'

'A fire-breathing dragon was tearing a village apart! The terrified villagers watched as the dragon destroyed their crops, devoured their sheep and tore down their markets. They looked on silently as the roofs of their homes were ripped off by its great wings. Then one day they woke up to find their children gone…'

Within these stories one gets a sense of how the staff of the organization felt and also how they reacted and responded to their daily struggles. The stories have very similar themes; feelings of loneliness, abandonment, being leaderless, lacking resources or direction, feeling powerless, overcome by adversity and at the mercy of others.

Images of an organization in crisis emerged that revealed some inner truths. On the surface it may look like stories are a good device to help to describe the organizational problems, in this case pointing clearly to issues of leadership and agency. But more than a problem-solving exercise they provide a window into the organization's soul.

Through metaphor, image and the poetry of the language, we are able to surface what is hidden and difficult to speak about. We struggle to talk openly and honestly about literal issues, but when we are given a metaphoric method it is easier to voice what lies hidden. Stories allow us to describe the problem in a language that is not hurtful but has a kind of honesty that we may struggle to find in normal language.

Stories help the 'unspeakable' to be spoken, to describe the indescribable

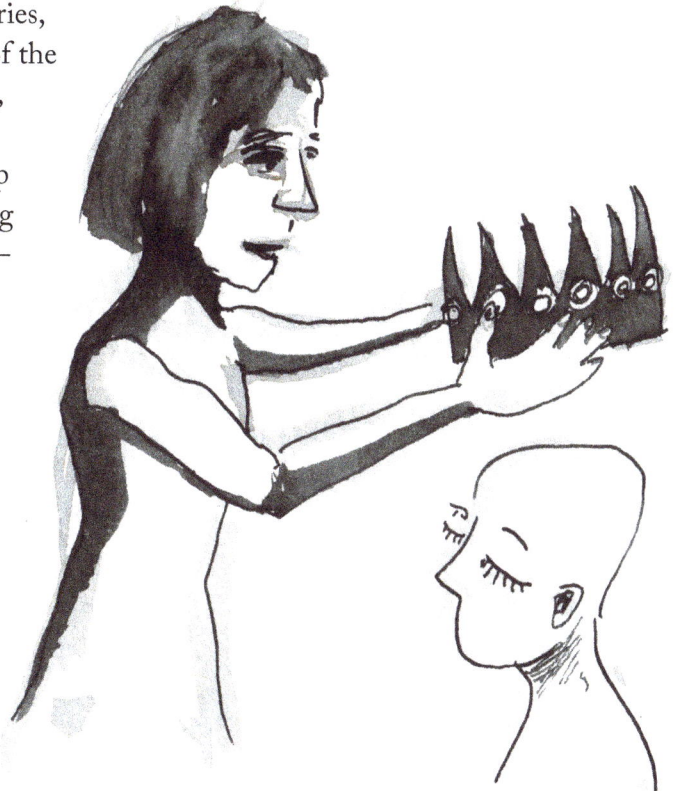

Through stories we can often get to the issue quite quickly, as the story can be short, succinct and focused.

But there is a further dimension that stories unlock. When we listen to a good story, we enter it in our imaginations and experience it vicariously, and through experiencing we can get closer to the truth in a more embodied way – we literally feel each other's stories. When we go beyond intellectual understanding to embodied empathetic knowing we also begin to connect with the will forces and what hinders the will to change, to engage with any fear, doubt or self-doubt or resentments that block our ability to see the truth and to change. That's the real power.

In early cultures, the storyteller and stories were at the heart of the tribe or group. The echo man, storyteller, shaman, griot, bard, elder and priest held and preserved the memories, identities and traditions of the people in an endless flow of stories. Through constant repetition and the weaving and circulation of these stories, songs and verses, an understanding of the world was brought in pictures, myths, metaphors and images.

The holder of the story helped to keep the entire system and community together, weaving together the history, truth, heroism, morality, love – wisdom.

Even today, stories are a powerful medium to bring us together and to help us understand ourselves. We all love stories because they are entertaining and engage all our senses, helping us to form strong images of our experiences and longings.

The fairy tale/folk tale, a traditional story format, can be used to understand the dilemmas that organizations and leaders face, as it carries within its structure truths that can provide common insights into human behaviour.

Fairy tales/folk tales often follow this sequence: There is a WOUND. Something that causes anguish or pain; a treasure has been stolen, a child is lost, a monster has taken the maiden, the village is under threat by a fire-breathing dragon. The wound is exposed. There is a crisis of the soul.

Then there is a journey, a WANDER, a leaving and a letting go. The journey is undertaken so that something can be seen anew, transformed or solved. The poor young man goes out to seek his fortune, the parents are searching in the deep forest to find the lost and loved child, the maiden looks for the hidden well, the courageous young woman climbs the misty mountain to face the dragon. It may be an inner or outer journey. It may be about trying to find the question as much as the answer.

For the organization or the leader, it is about bringing about change. It is about making the hidden visible. The journey is seeing with fresh eyes and exploring possible solutions. In breaking away from the past there can be an exploration of new and surprising unlearning and learning. It is here that the transformation with self and the world is possible.

At the end there is WONDER, when the soul is restored, and everything is made whole again and a sense of wonder and happiness fills the air.

For the organization or the leader new possibilities for growth can be seen. In the cameo stories from my organization, a few insights emerged: the organization was dealing with a wound or many wounds. These wounds were seen in the lost child, the floating raft, the hungry children, the shipwreck, the fire-breathing dragon, etc. Through the organizational process, the staff needed to go on a journey. We began to wander... to look outward at what was limiting us, hindering our work and threatening our livelihood and creativity. We could look inward and see our own hurts and limitations. It was in the journey carried by imaginative story and honest conversation, without blame or rancor, with deep reflection, sharing of ideas and asking new questions, that we could begin to rewrite and renew our organizational story. It was then that we could beat the dragon ...

In breaking away from the past there can be an exploration of new and surprising unlearning and learning

EMBRACING THE UNTAMED LIFE

The formal scheme was parasitic on informal processes that, alone, it could not create or maintain. To the degree that the formal scheme made no allowance for these processes or actually suppressed them, it failed both its intended beneficiaries and ultimately its designers as well.

Scott, James (1998) *Seeing like a State*, Yale University Press, New Haven and London, p.6

If an alien visited earth and asked you how the world works, you might easily begin by pointing out the *formal*, visible structures and rules created to give order to our lives – the economy, politics and dominant cultures. You might describe how our lives are shaped by the laws, policies, procedures, plans and protocols brought by a succession of mostly government and business leaders to drive or regulate our private and social interactions, in our businesses, our schools, the mass media and commercial culture, the workplace, neighbourhoods and families. You might describe the history and heroes, the struggles and sacrifices of great men and women that have led to the current state of affairs and the dynamics that are defining and shaping the road ahead.

But this is seeing only a fraction of the drama, a shallow perspective of life from the outside in, rather than the inside out.

A bigger truth is that we all live an untamed life, some more than others, largely beyond the knowledge and reach of the formal system, where we are ourselves, as individuals and in community, living lives despite the formal structures and cultures that seek to define our identities and worth. Not even we fully notice or appreciate who we really are, as we are constantly schooled to see our pale reflections in the mirrors that the formal system puts up for us.

We are arguing here that the truest and deepest reality of life, of who we really are, lives in the *informal*, unfolding continuously in the world inside and between people, in our dynamic relationships and emotional lives, in the unconscious intentions, passions and antagonisms, in the mad moments when we feel free to be ourselves, in what is unsaid, but understood, and most significantly in the horizontal, human-to-human generosity and kindness we display to each other every day.

These are the life processes, the life forces that really make the world go around, that indirectly and unwittingly feed and prop up the parasitic formal structures (the ones we described to our alien friend), that we imagine prop up and define our lives.

A bigger truth is that we all live an untamed life

These are also the life forces that enable the immense and growing wealth of our global elite, the billionaires who are rapidly accumulating untold wealth while a growing underclass slides deeper into poverty. Do we imagine that the richest 1% have worked so hard to deserve all those riches? If not, then who has?

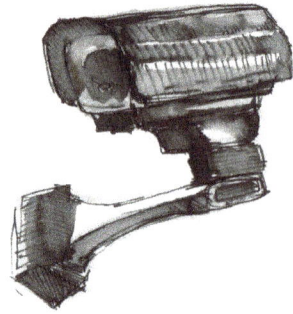

Scott, quoted above, is saying that the formal is not just subject to the informal but extractive, even parasitic of it, feeding off it, dependent on it for its own life, even while seeking to control or suppress it. This parasitic relationship is starkly illustrated, as he points out in the example of when trade unions call for "work-to-rule", when workers stick to the policies and procedures laid down by management, not using their initiative, and factories grind to an inflexible halt.

What about the true value to the world that "informal work" offers? Consider this fact from a recent Oxfam study[1]:

If all the unpaid care work done by women across the globe was carried out by a single company, it would have an annual turnover of $10 trillion, 27 to 43 times that of Apple.

It is no coincidence that this is largely work given to women, and that their contribution to preparing and supporting the formal workforce and the ballooning profits and fortunes of corporates and billionaires is missing from financial calculations.

> *We know the untamed life is there, we feel it, yet dismiss it in our visions and plans for a better world*

Yet the informal, untamed life, as the river that keeps all else afloat, is dimly perceived, without endorsement or value, apparently incidental to life, unacknowledged. We know the untamed life is there, we feel it and yet we dismiss it in our visions and plans for a better world.

Consequently, many leaders and managers imagine that their visible, clever and formally laid plans, their logical systems and structures are what shape and drive their world. When things do not work out as planned, they are often surprised and even angered, either with others for not sticking to the script or with themselves for not seeing what was really going on.

What they have not yet seen is the life-force of the untamed informal. What they have not figured into their calculations is that people (being people) are paradoxical, enigmatic and unpredictable. What they have experienced is culture confounding simplistic policies, of word-of-ear chatter and horizontal hearsay making mockery of the straight lines of communication they have carefully constructed to keep tabs on or control over who says what to whom.

Some leaders do learn their lessons when things go awry and start to work more artfully, anticipating the cultural unseen, even respecting it, and perhaps learning to consult and to craft their messages and strategies more tactfully.

But we are saying something more. The untamed life is not just some messy cultural mix of ordinary people being themselves despite the system.

What we bring to the world in informal expressions and cultural contributions, when we do not "work to rule", is a generosity of spirit and deed, whether intentional or not, that represents an immense life-force that almost literally 'makes the world go around'

We should not be so amazed by the generosity of spirit and the creative deeds of kindness of people that we witness and experience every day of our lives. But we are, because generosity seems to run against the tide, so counter to and despite the grand narratives where selfishness, profit- and status-seeking are acclaimed as the drivers of progress, of history itself. From Adam Smith to Ayn Rand to Donald Trump, society has been educated that it's OK to be selfish. We lead schizophrenic lives.

We lament the loss of that old culture of community and generosity, of mutual respect and circumspection, and we try to envision a future that restores these things. But I am beginning to wonder, in similar vein to Scott's quote, if the truth is that our modern economy and society is all the more extractive and parasitic and wholly dependent on a contemporary generosity and selflessness that still defines our human condition and motivation, today. We have not lost it at all. Our feet stand on its very ground. *Rather we have lost sight of it.*

In South Africa, since the turning of the tide in the 1990s, many of us, as white people, have been puzzled, but thankful and almost overwhelmed by the largesse and generosity of spirit shown by black people to their former oppressors, forgiving white people for unspeakable crimes and offering to walk side-by-side as human beings into the future, forgiving though not forgetting. The tragedy is that too many white South Africans do not appreciate the grace, the for-giving spirit of their fellow citizens, still imagining that black people need them more than they are needed. Tragically, many white people, who can afford to be generous, are the least so.

When we work in community, whether in organisations or neighbourhoods, it should not be difficult to see that the greatest asset that lives there is this neighbourly generosity and the love for each other that people have. It may not be visible to the naked eye, even obscured by the abuse and trauma that often accompanies poverty. But it is there, everywhere, every day between family members or neighbours, between friends and even strangers.

Do you know that the poor give to the poor in far greater amounts of quantifiable neighbourly aid to survive than is ever given by the Foundations of 'heroic' billionaires and aid agencies?

A study published on "The Philanthropy of the Poor"[2] reveals that the poor give to the poor in far greater amounts of quantifiable neighbourly aid to survive than ever given by the generous Foundations of heroic billionaires and the aid agencies of the Development Industry. This does not even account for the kind words, the sympathetic ear, the supportive mobilizations, and the empowering encouragements that cannot be priced or measured. Without these quantifiable and unquantifiable generosities, not only might communities collapse but so too would the economies and societies that depend on healthy workers turning up for work each day to keep the wheels turning and the tills ringing.

Between the unpaid mothers who raise the workers who make the billions of billionaires possible, who should be thankful to whom?

HOW DO GENERATIVE LEADERS EMBRACE THE UNTAMED LIFE?

In development-speak, this barely recognized untamed life would be oddly named 'local assets' or 'social capital' but it represents a real life-force that we must connect with if we wish to work with what people really have and are, and to do so respectfully and in solidarity. Human resourcefulness of generosity, love and kindness, alive in almost every human being, however hidden and misunderstood, is always there to be brought forward to shape the future.

Our most difficult task may be with those who have most lost sight of their own humanity. The rich and powerful who think they have no need for horizontal generosity of human beings, though they owe their millions and billions to it, is perhaps where the real development challenge lies, a capacity deficit that will take all the ingenuity we have to fill.

A key implication for those, from government or business, who are trying to spend the billions under their control for good, is to tread carefully to not disrupt the existing priceless relations of horizontal generosity between people everywhere. When this generosity turned into a political force, we know that it can be unstoppable. How can they see and enhance this, when it is so easy to diminish and replace it in destructive and unsustainable ways? There may be few more important challenges facing leaders of the world today.

All of this suggests that leaders have a real challenge to see and appreciate the untamed, hidden life and the deep resourcefulness of the people they lead. But just as we don't see this life, we often also miss the presence and significance of informal leaders who most fully embody this quality and are best placed to more consciously connect to and mobilize this resourcefulness for the common good – they are doing it already. Consider this quote from Meas Nee[3], a Cambodian development practitioner:

There are respected and good-hearted informal leaders in every village I have seen. They have hopes for peace and for restoring the life of their village. If they recognize the same qualities in the community development workers who befriend the village they will enlist our help. They will begin to show us that there is a way forward despite the problems. If we win their respect, we will be invited into their company. The changes that they can support are usually quite different from the changes that may be imposed by the district or the commune or the village leader.

Despite the unique context from which this observation originates, many readers will recognize that its wisdom applies to many contexts. Informal leaders work within the informal systems of the community. With intuitive insight they can see or feel what is really happening around them, forces that are seldom visible to the formal leader, and it is out of this capacity that they are able to act with wisdom.

These are the leaders and leadership impulses that provide the most valuable opportunities for reshaping the formal structures and resources of the world around the vast, untapped resourcefulness inside people and communities, to serve the continuation of life itself rather than its exploitation.

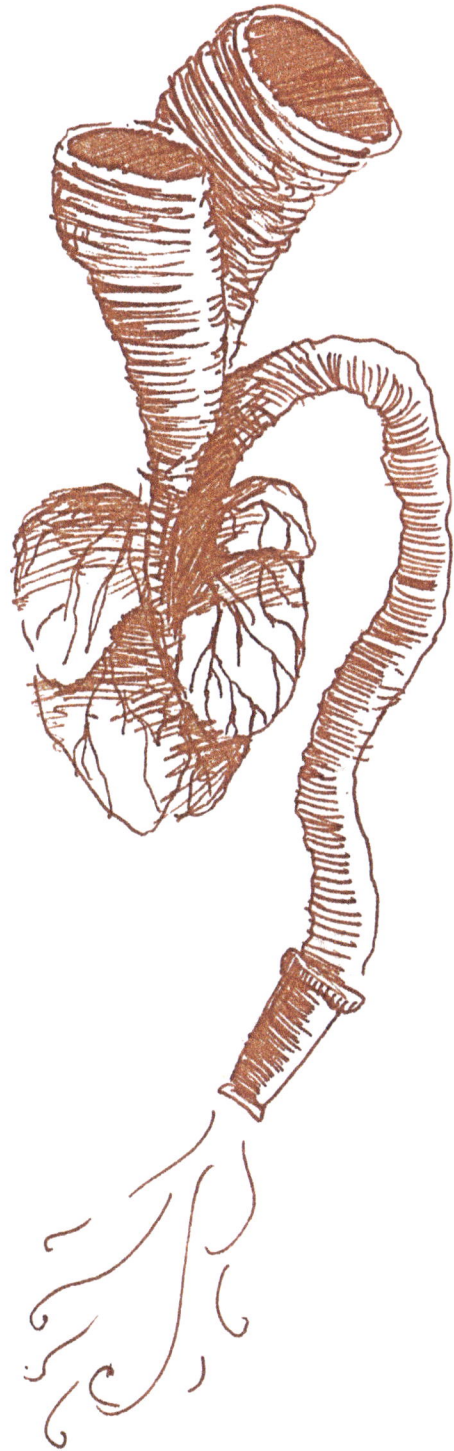

With intuitive insight they can see or feel what is really happening around them, forces that are seldom visible to the formal leader – out of this capacity they are able to act with wisdom

COMMUNITY DEFENDERS

CITIZEN-LED ACCOUNTABILITY

It's mid-afternoon. Retired police officer Armando Peláez stands outside a clinic in the village of Santa María, in San Pedro Jocopilas, Guatemala. It's closed, but it shouldn't be. There are no other health care services available for at least six thousand people living in this remote area.

Peláez has driven on many long dusty roads to get here. He remains still, looking at his surroundings, seeking an explanation. He acts like a detective but that's not why he is here. No, he wears a vest that identifies him not as a policeman but as a "community healthcare defender". He carries a notebook, a pen, and a form he's using to launch a formal complaint against the Ministry of Health.

He looks at his watch, it's 3:30 pm, and he's thinking: "It's not closing time yet. Not yet." A sign on the door says two auxiliary nurses are away and will be back for patients. But they are not back, and it doesn't look as if they will be. Villagers have told him that the health outpost is providing poor service and that's what he wants to know about. He writes everything down so he can report on it. He still wants to talk to the nurses, to ask them how much medicine is in stock, what supplies are missing, what infrastructure is needed, the number of people who get sick at a specific time and place, and how home visits are carried out.

He decides to come back the next day.

[From Guatemala's public healthcare defenders, by Oswaldo J. Hernández (photos: Sandra Sebastián, translated by: Louisa Reynolds), Crónicas No-Ficción No.1, May 2017, Guatemala City, Guatemala]

Guatemala has no formal mechanisms for citizens to demand their right to healthcare. Patients have no way to hold public healthcare employees accountable. Negligence is met with impunity and silence. For this reason, Walter Flores, director of the Center for the Study of Equity and Governance in Health Systems (CEGGS), helped found the network of community defenders.

Patients have no way to hold public healthcare employees accountable. Negligence is met with impunity and silence

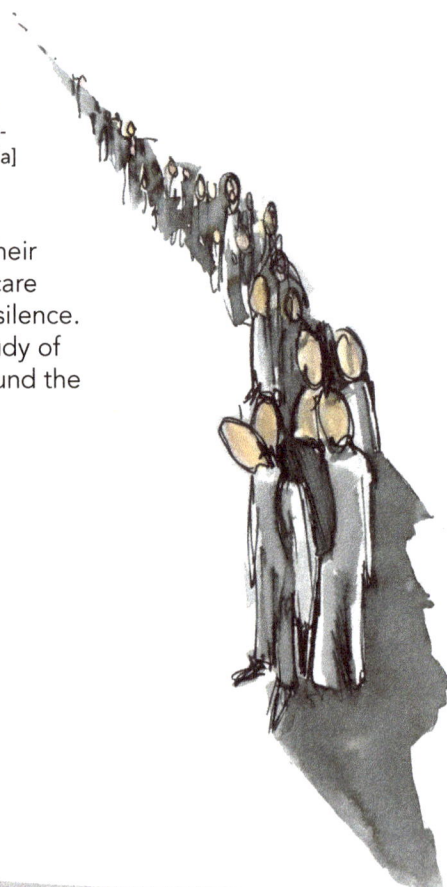

Community defenders are people who engage in independent and autonomous citizen action. They use whatever existing legal frameworks they can to build Rights Literacy campaigns amongst the community. They monitor public policies and services and demand accountability from authorities. They practice strategic advocacy to engage with the State at whatever level they can, even the national Parliament, Judiciary system, National Ombudsman and others.

They help people in local communities to move from passive users of services to active citizens that demand accountability

They collect audio-visual evidence, hold public exhibits of what they find or call press conferences, meet with parliamentarians, and present their evidence to public authorities.

Armando Peláez is a member of a network of community defenders who engage in independent and autonomous citizen action. He is one of over 120 people in 43 of Guatemala's 340 municipalities who track what is going on in a community, do advocacy work with local and even regional and national authorities, help the community hold accountable those who are supposed to serve them—and support those who serve when they are overburdened or themselves unsupported by their higher authorities.

The members of the Network of Healthcare Defenders know the people and the places where they go. They are not strange outsiders. So, they are trusted, and they can gather information that would not be shared with outsiders whose agendas are unclear or perhaps threatening. They are respected. They support each other, especially when confronted by hostile authorities who might fear what they expose. It's not light and easy work. It's tough. But their experience in Guatemala is that where, once healthcare professionals know what the Network of Healthcare Defenders is there for, they regard it as an ally that will listen to their complaints and provide support.

As Oswaldo J. Hernández who wrote the report on them says, "Healthcare defenders are not superheroes but the fact they're trying to save lives, is heroic in itself. ... The role they play means exercising the right to citizenship. Demanding the right to healthcare. We could all become community defenders." Community Defenders' journeys lead them to dangerous places for the good of all. Many of them live effectively in many different worlds or cultures within their own communities; they are what we call boundary leaders and will explore further in our next section.

BOUNDARY LEADERSHIP

We have mentioned 'boundary leaders' already. Boundary leaders are found in any and every community or group, especially where and when things are tough and need to change. Not necessarily those we usually call 'leaders,' they are crucial for change organizations. Here's why …

A boundary leader looks *beyond*, and works *across*, the boundaries of life most of us are too afraid to cross – racial, gendered, economic, disciplinary, institutional, or other similar boundaries – to see if something better can emerge by doing so. It's an approach to life, not a skill, a willingness to move into the spaces between boundaries, the 'boundary zones.'

This is where 'official' lines of authority are not working or are hurting people; where boxed in definitions of how and why to live restrict wholeness and well-being. Here a boundary leader recognizes where things can come together for good, where what appears to be disconnected can be connected to generate new and hopeful action.

For boundary leaders, the world is not only broken, but breaking open new in ways that allow for wholeness to emerge

Relationships in boundary zones tend to be fluid, dynamic, and in motion. That can be very uncomfortable, because boundary leaders are not intent on defining and policing boundaries. Not stuck inside the spaces or borders made by others or by the official lines of control, ownership, naming, and accountability, they often don't feel fully appreciated by the institutions for which they work. They often feel alone, or in awkward relationship to those whose bonds or identities seem threatened or who can't understand why they are moving in a different, newer path.

Yet a boundary leader is able to hold these tensions creatively together, to stand in-between, not just apart from, those identities and bonds. Transforming others, willing to risk life on the edge, they experience that transformation themselves: greater self-knowledge, greater awareness of others, an ability to empathize with others and take a critical perspective on their own position, institution, community, society or tradition.

And they aren't really alone either. Other boundary leaders, though one might not recognize them at first, are around who share this journey. Here one finds friendship, collegiality and guidance into the boundary zones just when it is needed most.

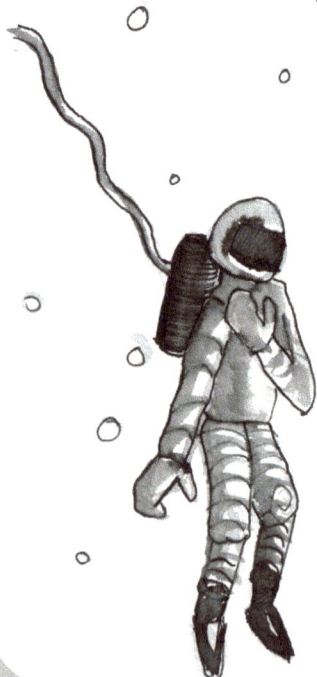

THE FIVE MARKS OF BOUNDARY LEADERSHIP

We see in boundary leadership five important competencies that make up a common pattern to their lives in the social ecology within which they live and with which we can work (there's a **whole chapter** on this in *Barefoot Guide #3!*).

EMBRACING COMPLEXITY OF PERSONS AND SYSTEMS

Boundary leaders, because they are deeply engaged with other people and aware of the challenges and complexity of life in the real world, live into complex social realities without trying to simplify things. That makes for humility. It forces one to be sensitive to conflict, tension, and turmoil, and even unexpected personal transformation.

LIVING WITH MISUNDERSTANDING

Boundary leaders often feel misunderstood, suspected by their organizational structure or profession, and marginalized, invisible, under-valued, or even endangered professionally. So, they have complicated work journeys and, quite frequently, complicated job histories that may appear curious, or worrying, to those on more traditional paths.

CREATING BRIDGES AND KEEPING THEM OPEN

To cross boundaries, holding on to the whole and not letting any part go, means building bridges between people who stay within their boundaries. It's how one gets many things done that would be impossible otherwise—linking people with different things to offer, connecting energies that need to be connected. Because people often prefer to stay within their boundaries, or may fear those outside, once one has created a useful and meaningful bridge, a boundary leader also takes care to keep the bridge open.

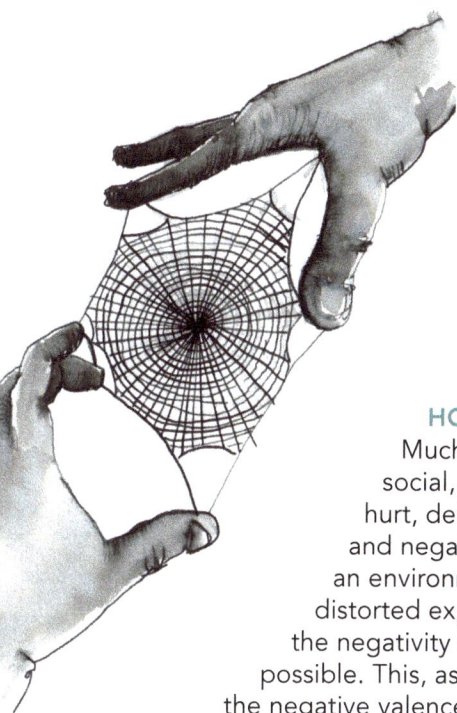

ENGENDERING WEBS OF TRANSFORMATION

Boundary leaders don't stop there. They also try to build new structures that will enable this to keep happening, so that what is gained in the process is not lost again. It's their nature to be part of a growing web of transformation that helps transform the social whole over the long haul, sustainably. That means working hard to keep people and groups together who share a common vision and aim for the well-being of all.

HOLDING THE NEGATIVE VALENCE

Much in boundary zones is broken, the debris of destructive social, political and economic processes that leave people hurt, dehumanized, depressed or damaged. Fear, mistrust, and negativity may dominate. A leader coming into such an environment can act as a lightning rod for unrealistic or distorted expectations. A boundary leader is able to deal with all the negativity while looking for the positive transformation that is possible. This, as counselors and psychologists know, is called 'holding the negative valence.'

AMOS HEALTH AND HOPE

Laura, a doctor and public health professional who lives and works in Nicaragua and fights for a world where everyone has the opportunity to make a fulfilling life choice, shares the story of her father-in-law, physician Gustavo Parajon. Founder in 2006 of a non-profit in Nicaragua to improve the "health of all," he is a truly generative boundary leader who easily traverses the worlds of church, medicine, government, politics, warring factions, and other stakeholders.

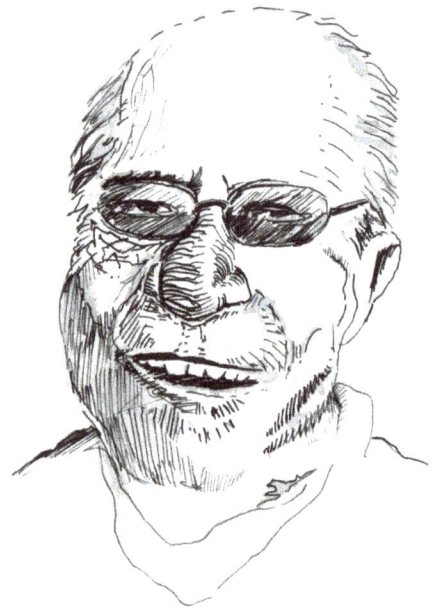

A BOUNDARY LEADER IN ACTION

Gustavo, a Baptist pastor and physician, grew up in Nicaragua the son of a pastor who brought together all the Baptist Churches of Nicaragua during the 1940s. With his mom and dad he travelled all over the country to visit churches, and saw there the suffering of the people with no health care. He also saw their strengths and their ability to find solutions to their own issues in the community. After studying at medical school in the U.S. he returned to his country to start its first immunization and community health worker program.

During his lifetime, he brokered the peace accords between the warring Sandinista and Contra party, helping to bury thousands of weapons in peace parks throughout Nicaragua. Over forty years he built relationships in communities all over Nicaragua, with church leaders of different denominations, with government officials, and with politicians, seeing each person as a partner and someone to learn from. These relationships became the seeds that started many non-profits dedicated to address the issues of social justice—peace for all, health for all, literacy for all, education for all, and sharing the good news of a loving God.

Gustavo was among those present in the famous Alma Ata meeting of the World Health Organization in the early 1980s. Here he helped it create the document on "Health for All" that ever since has inspired generations of socially minded health professionals trying to decrease health inequities. In Nicaragua this document has become a source of inspiration for many socially conscious community health practitioners. It gives them a foundation to learn from the past and the present and build for the future as they support communities and work for health for all.

'See the suffering but also the strengths and ability to find their own solutions of people in local communities'

Gustavo's legacy as a generative leader and man of deep faith carries over today in AMOS Health and Hope, a non-profit organization he helped found in 2006. The name is inspired by the prophet Amos whose focus on social justice and sensitivity to poor and marginalized populations inspired Gustavo's work both as a physician and a peacemaker. AMOS is now run by his son, Mark, and daughter-in-law, Laura, both also physicians. Its mission is to decrease health inequities by working alongside poor and marginalized populations in health, education, and development.

AMOS works with communities using the strategies of Community Based Primary Health Care (CBPHC) to train local community health workers (CHWs). They learn basic skills in healthcare provision and health promotion.

The CHWs are equipped with basic skills in community organizing and management of simple community clinics in places where there are no formally trained medical providers. And their own strengths they bring with them from their community experience and knowledge are identified and supported. AMOS also facilitates the integration of CHWs into the government health care system for long-term sustainability.

As a medical and health organization AMOS takes seriously the importance of the what of evidence-based interventions (such as neonatal home visitation to reduce neonatal mortality, or integrated management of childhood illnesses to decrease their death rates). But AMOS also believes that the *how* of approaching communities is just as important. This includes practicing cultural humility, strengths-based empowering methods, careful listening, and genuine collaboration.

Gustavo's favourite place to be at AMOS was in a circle of rocking chairs where he would chat with people—always starting with their lives, who they were, and what they were all about. The circle of rocking chairs was a symbol of everyone being equal and on the same level—no one over anyone, and everyone together as equals. He never imposed his views on others, he mostly listened and learned from them, and he helped them build their community, all while he shared his deep faith in the ability of all people to make a difference in this world. His aim was to bring people of all faiths, beliefs, and politics together to help build a future of mercy and justice.

Gustavo was gentle and kind but, convinced by Matthew 6:10 ("*Your kingdom come, your will be done on* **earth** *as it is in heaven*"), he was not one to wait patiently for "heaven" to arrive. He intended to live it out here on earth. He was inspired by the vision from Isaiah 65:

"Never again will there be in it an infant who lives but a few days or an old man who does not live out his years; the one who dies at a hundred will be thought a mere child."

So he set out to do what he could to help create a place where every child and every adult has the ability to have an abundant life and have it in the full, where no child dies of a preventable disease, and every elderly person and adult has the healthcare that they need. The ends he pursued and his determination to live them in his daily life and work to the best of his ability, not alone but with all people of good will, mark the generative leadership that still drives those who have followed him and lie at the root of the work and ministry at AMOS.

FOUR DIMENSIONS OF GENERATIVE WISDOM FOR GENERATIVE LEADERSHIP

As I sit down to write this, I feel overcome by the news that a good friend has been diagnosed with breast cancer, and then the news that 59 people were gunned down in Las Vegas just hours ago shakes me even more. This senseless act of violence is one of many that makes us all tremble to the core.

My friend recently ended her blog by referring to the hymn, *It is Well with my Soul*. In her short reflection that followed, she acknowledged that she longs for this "wellness," and trusts that it will come. However, in her plaintive longing, I hear a spark of wisdom that tells me that she is part of a much bigger story that continues to unfold. I am reminded of the Psalmist who says that *Wisdom calls to our depths and joins us with the story of the greater world*.

This depth of understanding of the world and one's place in it—a world that contains great suffering and great joy—a world threatened by the human capacity for evil but enriched by love and justice and mercy, a world full of unlimited possibility that will continue on even if we humans destroy life as we know it—calls for our wisdom in action.

How does generative leadership work from a source of wisdom, accessing, acknowledging and setting free the capacity for communities to choose love and justice and mercy? How might the language of wisdom guide us? How is wisdom a function of generative leadership? Is wisdom generative? If so, how?

Psychology Today suggests that '*wisdom is an integration of knowledge, experience and deep understanding that incorporates tolerance for the uncertainties of life as well as its ups and downs. It is an awareness of how things play out over time and confers a sense of balance—it conveys an ability to see the big picture, a sense of proportion and considerable introspection*'. What then are the key themes that help us understand what we can call generative wisdom?

> *Wisdom calls to our depths and joins us with the story of the greater world*

Generative wisdom, I feel, propels engagement with the world in constructive and necessary ways. It does this when it is grounded in four ways: In the knowledge and experience of abundance in creation, in the interdependence of all life, in the humility of knowing one's self and context, and in critical hope.

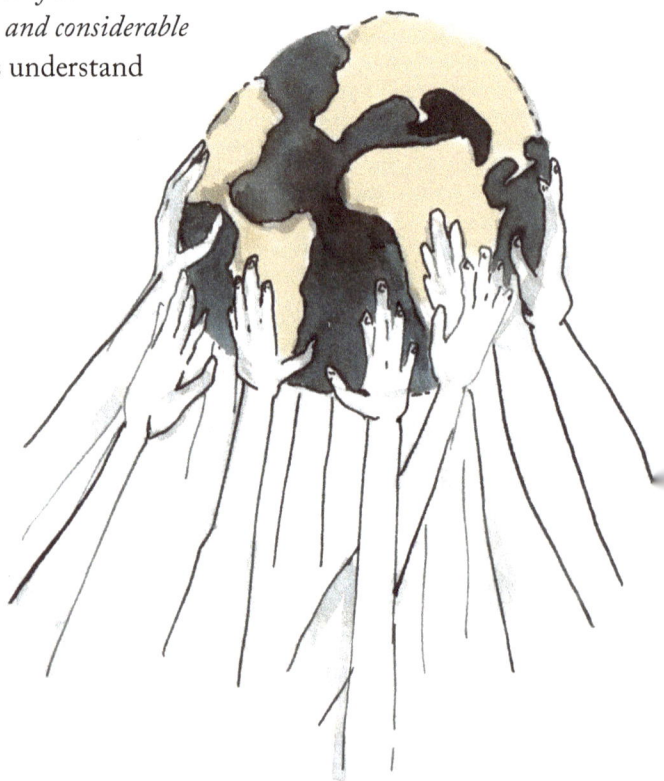

THE WISDOM OF ABUNDANCE

The world is fraught with issues of scarcity—food, water, resources. People are dying of hunger, disease, violence and from environmental disasters due to climate change. How might I even begin to claim that there is abundance in this world? Those who live with power and privilege—individuals, like me, institutions, systems, nations—tend to hoard resources and accumulate material goods in an attempt to assuage the fear of scarcity. Human consumption is testing the limits of our planet. Those of us with economic and political power often end up blocking access to resources and abusing the resources we have. Generative wisdom remains attentive to how the fear of scarcity shows up and shapes our actions and policies. The wisdom of abundance allows room for creative possibilities and trusts that there is more than enough available. Generative wisdom is vigilant about responding from a place of abundance.

I am reminded of one of our Faith Health Fellows who was struggling to find meals for elderly patients being discharged from the hospital who could not cook for themselves. She discovered that there were skilled care/assisted living facilities that were throwing out food that was not used. In conversation, she found that the facility could not give food to her or to volunteers to be distributed outside of the building due to regulations. However, those who were in marketing from that organization could—they could be trusted to follow the regulations necessary to give the food. Thus, the marketers now deliver food to elderly individuals in their homes. Where there once seemed to be no solution—a mutually beneficial arrangement emerged. Evidence of abundance in action. Where suffering exists is where human beings have failed to grant everyone access to this abundance.

Personal and professional stories also fuel my understanding of abundance. The first comes from my experience as an educator. I once had a student who claimed to be quite sick—terminally ill. I was devastated and overwhelmed by her potential death. It became apparent over a couple of years of ups and downs with her, that I did not know the full story. Many people doubted her illness, as did I. After personal reflection and consultation about my anger (first at her illness and then at her), sadness, frustrations and worries, I realized I was operating from a place of scarcity. First, the pain of her potential death was heartbreaking. Then I couldn't bear to give my time to someone who seemed to be lying about her illness. I didn't have enough time/love/energy to share.

The wisdom of abundance allows room for creative possibilities and trusts that there is more than enough available

After reflection, I realized that she seemed to want just a little attention. Where I once felt she wanted more than I could ever offer, I recognized that I had enough. Once I reached that place of abundance with her, I could show up, be fully present, without expectation, without a need for clarity, without anger and frustration. The wisdom of abundance granted me access to generosity and patience. Once I moved past scarcity, I began to trust that she would find healing when she was ready—not in my time, but in hers, which she did.

Abundance creates a spirit of generosity which simply reinforces a sense of abundance—From a place of abundance, communities and individuals can respond with a sense that there is time for relationship, there is time to attend to conflict, there are resources to be accessed and shared ... The wisdom of abundance fosters responsiveness versus reactiveness. In my experience as a chaplain, I have entered into deeply distressing times full of chaos and fear and despair. In these times, the best gifts have not been words. In anxious times, people need a calm space in the storm where they are seen and heard. Wisdom knows and trusts this deeply. A sense of abundance allows for this space. This does not have to deny the urgency the moment. In fact, generative wisdom holds the paradox that there is both ultimate abundance and here-and-now urgency/scarcity. This wisdom holds the truth of Julian of Norwich's words that "All shall be well, and all shall be well and all manner of thing shall be well" and acknowledges the 'not yet' of those words.

From a place of abundance, communities and individuals can respond with a sense that there is time for relationship, there is time to attend to conflict, there are resources to be accessed and shared ...

As a mother, I have a glimpse of the limitless, abundant capacity of love. I had no idea I could love others so deeply. Generative wisdom is grounded in this belief of the abundance of love. A love that is fierce and indefatigable—a love that believes that there is more than enough to go around and works to ensure all have access to the abundance that is there. Generative wisdom constantly reminds people of the abundance of this creation while recognizing the work it takes to create access to this abundance.

I have seen the wisdom (discipline) of abundance in action through the work of Gary Gunderson, who consistently fights the insidious model of scarcity in the hospital. His refusal to fall prey to scarcity helped him to see assets where others hadn't—he was able to convince the board of the hospital foundation to use foundation funds for smart charity. Access to those funds allowed the division to move more proactively into community while also attracting more funds from other foundations. The wisdom of abundance is attractive because it gives generously of resources and time. It asks little of others, but others respond to it generously and willingly. The spirit of abundance of this leader led to relatively rapid engagement of individuals within multiple health systems—this wisdom recognizes that we never know where the next meeting might lead and trusts that the potential for new assets and resources is always possible ...

The question remains—how does a sense of abundance inform the urgency of need in the world? What balances this? Is it fierce love that demands attention to the urgent? What about those communities who are stuck in systems of oppression which perpetuate real scarcity of resources—is a grounding in abundance a realistic expectation—is it meaningful at all?

What practices encourage a grounding in abundance? Certainly, self-awareness of what scarcity stirs in us as individuals and communities …

THE WISDOM OF INTERDEPENDENCE

There is no such thing as other people's children.
Glennon Doyle Melton

White western individualism is the source of great brokenness in my culture. The tribalism and xenophobia supported by individualism leaves communities fragmented and disenfranchised. The quote above speaks to the heart of the matter. As a mother, what I want for my own children is what I want for all children. This was driven home more deeply to me by the image of Alan Kurdi, the 3-year-old Syrian boy who drowned when his family made the treacherous journey to find safety in a new country. No child, no mother, no one should face this fate—and yet we do, because we have forgotten our interdependence.

We forget that we belong to each other. As a mother, I find myself feeling more compassion than I ever did before. I remember being with a rather irritating student following my maternity leave. At some point in my conversation, it suddenly came to me that he was once someone's little boy. In that moment, I connected with a level of compassion that I had yet to experience. This led to a much deeper engagement and meaningful relationship.

Human beings have divided the world into us and them, in and out. Interdependence demands that all are included and speaks the truth to power regarding the marginalized and oppressed. Reverend William Barber, a pastor from North Carolina, models this in his renewal and revitalization of the Poor People's Campaign. He insists in action and language a commitment to all who are oppressed—he has shown up to protest the closure of hospitals in rural white communities, protested racism across the country, and shown up to speak for immigrants at deportation hearings. He does not allow the polarization of our country to separate him from the common struggles that exist among all poor. He sees how we are all connected and persistently calls each of us to see the same.

As Martin Luther King, Jr. once said, "Injustice anywhere is a threat to justice everywhere"

I am struck by the wisdom of our creation whose health depends on diversity

Generative wisdom acknowledges the depths of interconnectivity and interdependence of all life. It sees into the necessity of diversity for survival and creative possibilities. I am struck by the wisdom of our creation whose health depends on diversity.

Thus, I believe that generative leadership requires vigilant attention to the impact of our decisions— who is included in the decision-making process, who identifies the question, how do decisions impact those with the least power? Interdependence trusts that what is best for the least of these us ultimately best for all. A murmuration of starlings exemplifies the interdependence of community. As Archbishop Desmond Tutu shared, "All humanity is dependent upon recognizing the humanity in others."

The minute that I dehumanize another, my own humanity is diminished. This came home painfully earlier this year following conversations with my children about Martin Luther King, Jr. and the challenges that African Americans face in our culture. I worked to explain how in the U.S. the colour of our white skin grants us more unearned and unfair privileges. Thus, we have a greater responsibility to notice, name and share our privileges with others.

A week later, my daughter said, "Mom, I wish all people were white." I was horrified. After some conversation, I realized from her innocent mind, she felt that if everyone looked the same, then there wouldn't be inequality. Since white skin granted more privileges in our culture, in her mind, everyone should be white. This was an understandable stance from the perspective of a little white girl whose mother told her white skin gave people more privileges.

I realized then that I had failed in helping her to see the beauty of anyone whose skin isn't white. My internalized racism cost my children a wide vision of beauty and insight into what they might have to learn from those who don't look like them. I am still learning and trying.

What does this look like on the ground? What are the practices that foster awareness of our interdependence?

THE WISDOM OF HUMILITY

Generative wisdom includes deep humility that recognizes and honours the gifts of others. It keeps an eye out for, believes that there is and highlights the 'Fynbos'[4] in community. It holds space for that beauty to emerge. Over the course of this week, I've been grateful for the leaders here who pointed out the exquisite beauty of tiny flowers in the wild that I may have missed. There is stunning (abundant) beauty all around—it often just takes time and patience to see.

Often power structures fail to see the innate beauty in those on the ground. Two leaders from my past, Rev. Ramona Prestwood (from childhood) and Chaplain Richard McBride (college) were both quiet yet skillful in noticing and encouraging my gifts.

They were humble in their own lives and sought to always lift up others in their midst. Their generative wisdom taught me the importance of sharing power. They lived in ways that helped me to find my own answers to my own questions—they did not impose their will and assumptions on me, but rather trusted my inner wisdom to guide me.

From them I learned that no one person, institution, community, etc., holds all wisdom—there is always more to be learned. This humility "trusts the process," including states of dis-equilibrium, and holds space for greater wisdom to emerge.

I believe that generative wisdom is humble because it is grounded in personal and communal stories and understands the strengths and limits of individuals and community. Humble leaders acknowledge their mistakes and failure. I think that humility also recognizes that there are more stories and more perspectives to be held and honoured. I was raised in a family of strong, independent, opinionated, faithful southern women—Steel Magnolias. There was always a right way of being in the world (often this way was loving and thoughtful).

Often power structures fail to see the innate beauty in those on the ground

Early on, I internalized this mindset and a sense of a responsibility (as an eldest child) for others. It was hard not to pass judgement on and impose my beliefs on those who were different when I first left home. However, as I got to know friends from all backgrounds, I was humbled by their love and beauty, by how they made sense of the world, and I felt the grace of recognizing my own limits in understanding and how much I had (and still have) to learn. It is one of the many reasons I was drawn to ministry.

I believe that humility acknowledges the need for, asks for and accepts help. Humility is grounded in recognizing that one human being, even one community, is a small part of the greater story of all of creation. It's a bit like being the center person of the group of three in the figure 8 movement in our morning eurythmy session. It was humbling for me to see the movement and gifts of those on either side and recognize that I was not in control or leading, but rather one of the team. I sometimes felt crowded, sometimes concerned about those moving at different speeds, sometimes held. Humility invites critical reflection on all the perspectives emerging—noting who holds the power, who is being left out, where there is abundance, where the fear of scarcity is showing up, etc.

WISDOM AS CRITICAL HOPE

Generative wisdom recognizes and values the role of critical hope in work that can be exhausting, never-ending and full of despair. When one's work seems to move three steps forward and two steps back, when progress is difficult to see or hold in sight, when meanness seems to win, when community is messy and slow, when people are still dying in spite of abundance, it is hard, if not impossible, for me to remain hopeful. Augustine of Hippo is credited with saying, "Hope has two lovely daughters, anger and courage." I think critical hope asks that I give space to my anger and leverage that anger (with courage) through constructive action. This often starts with an invitation to name anger and hurt.

As a chaplain, I have seen that critical hope demands that suffering and pain and fear be named and lamented. It requires that space be created for ritual and meaning-making in a senseless world. Human beings need time and space to make sense of their world and to name that which will never make sense.

Augustine of Hippo is credited with saying, "Hope has two lovely daughters, anger and courage"

Critical hope bears witness by recognizing that the only way out is through. Embracing and creating ritual harnesses the power of agency that can create space for movement in stuck and seemingly hopeless times. For those devastated by the election of Donald Trump, actions like participation in protests and marches, writing letters, making phone calls were rituals that helped people access some sense of agency in this out of control world. For my friend, writing a blog post about her cancer and hitting the post button leveraged her agency in the world—it created space for hope. From the beautiful lamentation ritual planned with leadership from TC, people were given space to speak aloud or silently the pain that they carried and then moved into dancing. This is the constructive action of ritual.

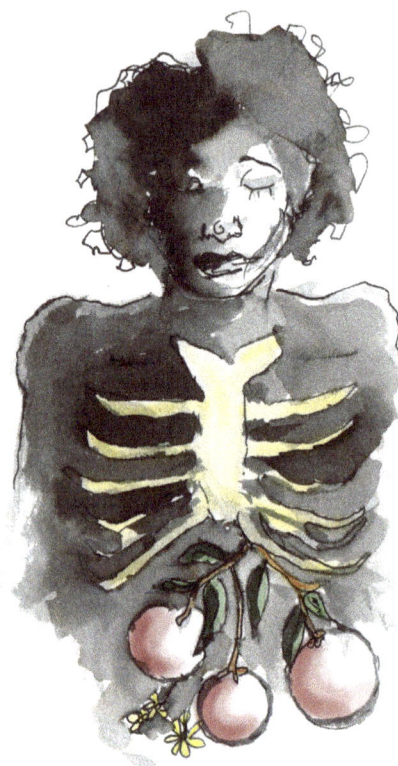

Critical hope is also always on the lookout for progress in even the smallest measures of success. These, too, are named and honoured. As Mary Oliver reminds us "Instructions for living a life. Pay attention. Be astonished. Tell about it." Critical hope "tells about it" whatever "it" is. Rev. William Barber fosters critical hope by reminding us that we have been through dark times before—today is a new incarnation of past challenges through which we are called to forge once again. As one of the earliest quotes from our meeting stated, "It will all be okay in the end and if it is not okay it is not the end." A poem by Padraig O'Tuama speaks a similar theme:

NARRATIVE THEOLOGY #1

And I said to him:
Are there answers to all of this?
And he said:
The answer is in a story and the story is being told.
And I said:
But there is so much pain

And she answered, plainly, Pain will happen.
Then I said:
Will I ever find meaning?
And they said:
You will find meaning
where you give meaning.
The answer is in a story and the story isn't finished.

Critical hope reminds us that the story isn't finished—there is more plot, more narrative. Generative wisdom creates space for new narrative to emerge.

Critical hope reminds us that the story isn't finished—there is more plot, more narrative

Generative wisdom fosters critical hope by constantly reminding people and community of their better natures, of abundance, of interdependence. Sometimes this takes great imagination—it always demands time and space for reflection. This critical hope inspires people to see what is possible without losing sight of what is real now.

GENERATIVE INSIGHT: OBSERVING THE WHOLE RIVER

"None of the human faculties should be excluded from scientific activity. The depths of intuition, physical exactitude, the heights of reason and sharpness of intellect together with a versatile and ardent imagination, and a loving delight in the world of the senses—they are all essential for a lively and productive apprehension of the moment."

Johann Wolfgang von Goethe

The first challenge of leadership is to look for and to see things as they really are, in their essence, not just the surface skin but fully as they are. Sit on the bank of a river and observe what makes the river. You can see not just the water, but the banks, what flows around and under, the trees, grasses, fish and insects. All part of the living system we call river. The river is also upstream, its origins, and downstream, its journey and destination. Ask yourself how much of the river you can see. Just the skin. Even if the riverbed is partially visible in front of you there is more river below and beyond that, seeping through the soils and sands, slower and deeper and invisible. And in there is more life, invisible micro-organisms but teeming.

We can assemble a list of a river's constituent parts, water, earth, plants, animals. We can list them and lay them out on a table, each part with its specific properties. But this is a fragmented, piece-meal and obvious picture, a lifeless assembly of objects. This is conventional science using our faculties of direct observation and logical analysis. But we know the river is much more than this. How? We have another faculty that takes these observed pieces and weaves them into a living picture. Our imaginations, our ability to bring things that we cannot see out there into a picture that lives in our minds, a living picture that tells a story. Even hard-nosed scientists cannot help themselves doing this. They must make assumptions, and in making these assumptions, however well-tested, they are imagining something they cannot see. Almost all knowledge is held in this way. Through imaginative insight we connect the pieces we see into living pictures and begin to grasp and appreciate the life that moves beyond our sight.

This is certainly better, but it can still be mechanical, an imagined articulation of the different elements. To see deeper we can go further through an act of bolder imagination. We can begin to look for the relationships between things, and gradually another, truer and whole river, might arise in our mind's eye.

Through imaginative insight we connect the pieces we see into living pictures and begin to grasp and appreciate the life that moves beyond our sight

"The beginning is pure observation, over time, across parts, to begin to see patterns, threads, wholes rather than parts, relationships. Eventually, if we are 'lucky', we will fall into the river. And the trick then is to stay dry despite being immersed and be able to climb in and out at will."

Allan Kaplan[5]

We can try to become its elements and flows and connections, to experience, even to embody the river and in that process not to just "objectively" observe the life but feel it too and in that to see a truth or essence of the life forces at play, indeed to appreciate the unique life it holds and where it is wanting to go. To be immersed but not swallowed.

In the same way that we can imaginatively see into the life of a river, we can do the same in the social realm. Indeed, we do it all the time. We do it through a deeper form of imagination, a compassionate, even loving capacity we call empathy. Through empathetic listening we enter each other's experience and begin to deeply understand. We have to imagine things we cannot see, not by whimsical invention (that is a danger) but through compassionate intuition. For those "scientists" who worry about objectivity, this kind of exercise, when done consciously, goes beyond both subjectivity and objectivity (as either/or lenses) to a field of observation where the truth is revealed precisely because there is loving intention, not despite it.

Generative leaders can do the same by seeing an organization as a social being. Through observation of its patterns, its moving wholeness, through feeling and listening to the questions that emerge we can "fall into" the organization, holding in ourselves its living and breathing interactions and in so doing better understand, through our experiencing, what its deeper experiencing is and where it is going, and even through empathetic embodiment, feeling where its life or will forces are moving or are constrained. This takes us to where the real work is.

"I would love to live like a river flows,
carried by the surprise of its own unfolding."
– John O'Donohue –

CHAPTER 5

LIVING IN THE RIVER
Aspects of a Leader's Being

The river lives and moves, carrying with it the past, moving through the present and heading into the future. As it meanders over rocks, pebbles and vegetation, it is always 'becoming', always changing and pushing towards the end, the wide-open sea of possibility. So too the turbulence which the river experiences is part of its being, its life.

In the previous chapter we spoke about practicing generative leadership in turbulent times. Now we are asking what carries the leader forward? What are the attitudes or approaches needed to help generative leadership flourish? What does it mean to "be" a leader? And what kind of people are we when we are most generative?

Kirsten and two colleagues discuss 'generative leadership' and some of the ideas presented so far.

[Kirsten] We've said a few times that being a *generative* leader has little to do with skills, techniques, methods, or even special gifts (that 'charisma'). Those may be useful in their place, but more important is *how we live, how we bring ourselves* in the streams of life we seek to lead. We have seen that this has a lot to do with the 'ends' we serve. Indeed, there is a unity between the ends and our being that we need to be conscious of.

[Leo]   Are you saying that they are the same thing?

[Kirsten] Well, they are certainly integrated, in other words there is integrity between what we are pursuing and how we bring ourselves. When we experience that integrity in someone who is leading then it is generative to everyone—it stirs life, hope and courage. You know this. And if that integrity is missing, if the lofty intentions expressed by leaders are not matched by how they are experienced as people, then the opposite happens, where energy, indeed the life-force inside and between people, can dissipate or even die. Insincerity and hypocrisy can be profoundly demoralizing. But this can also be true for heroic leaders. Generative leadership is both different and goes much further.

> *When people experience integrity in someone who is leading then that is generative to all around—it stirs life, hope and courage*

[Leo]   OK, that sounds interesting, but explain it more practically.

[Kirsten] At the heart of the work is not playing the hero or saviour, like bringing the vision, the energy or brilliant solutions. We may experience heroes and saviours as great leaders, but they can also bring a great shadow over us, making our own leadership irrelevant, disempowering us in their glory. Generative leadership is quite the opposite. Can you see that?

[Leo] Well, I feel relieved that I don't have to be a hero! But it's not that clear what I do have to be as a generative leader.

[Li Wei] In some ways I guess it's much less work and in some ways it's more! It's about paying attention to two things at the same time: what's alive and awake within an individual, community or organization with which we are working, and how to encourage and support that, including everyone's leadership potential, while also focusing on the forces from the past and in the present which serve to suppress or diminish that life. People are lively, energetic beings, with a natural vitality, of intelligence, a deeply social empathy for each other and a powerful, innate urge to create. It's in our DNA!

[Leo] But this is often blocked by the trauma and distress of historical and current experiences of things like racism, sexism and other kinds of domination, subjugation or exclusion—both as victims and as perpetrators.

[Kirsten] Oh, no doubt. Our human vitality can be so easily sapped by experiences that produce things like fear, self-doubt or hatred and even self-hatred. How can people be liberated from these things? This question is central to generative leadership.

[Li Wei] OK so, what you are saying is essentially about paying attention to where life or vitality is, and strengthening it, as well as paying attention to what is hindering our vitality, and helping to free it up. And you are saying that this is both the ends and the means? I think I am getting this! It feels more and more like we are dealing with a kind of 'culture of leadership' that everyone can be a part of!

[Kirsten] That's a good way of putting it. Let's explore some aspects of a generative culture of leadership and work with them.

People are lively, energetic beings, with a natural vitality, of intelligence, a deeply social empathy for each other and a powerful, innate urge to create. It's in our DNA!

LIVING IN TIME AND SPACE, BEING PRESENT

What we want to focus on are certain ways of thinking about how time and space affect a culture of generative leadership, as well as the kind of "persona" or ways of being we can adopt that help us live it out. Knowing that the effects of the past, the possibilities of the present, and what we hope for in the future all affect us deeply. It will help if we are clear about three things in particular.

1. No matter what and where you lead, *you did not create what came before you.* Others from the past left you something to work with. But not only in the past! *You are also always only one actor in the present*, alongside many others who act and lead in their own right. Acknowledging those from the past upon whom you build and those from the present who build with you is the first crucial thing. And it's really surprising how easy it is to forget this. As soon as you do remember it you open yourself up to a living web of human beings, their history and traditions, their interests and needs, their desires and aspirations.

2. *You cannot determine the consequences of your actions.* Put differently, you can't control the future and, whatever your intentions, things can and often do, turn out otherwise. For positional leaders it's normal to have some control over things for which you are given authority. But many make the mistake of thinking they can or should control everything and, even worse, that they have the right to do so. That's exactly when they lose flexibility, sensitivity, adaptability, and, in the end, a hold on things. Of course, to consider the consequences of what you do or say is simply being wise, and that's not trivial. But real wisdom means being aware of what you *don't* control and learning how to work with that, especially learning from what happens, continually, so that you can adapt and negotiate the turbulence.

> *Real wisdom means being aware of what you don't control and learning how to work with that*

3. *You can control your intentions.* Specifically, you can control what motivates your leadership, what you ultimately aim at in your leadership, and how you will live that out to the best of your capabilities no matter what. This is at the heart of *being* a generative leader.

So, having said all that, let's look at some ways of approaching time, space, and persons in relation to *being* a generative leader.

ARTISTRY IN THE LIVED MOMENT ~ "PLAYING WITH INFINITY"

Liz's story: Whatever past or future means for us, it's the present, 'lived' moment in which we decide how to live and what for. During the writing of this Barefoot Guide, as a Eurythmy facilitator, I introduced the group to some of its elements to help us all become conscious of how our location in a particular space and moment shapes the 'lived moment,' which I call "*playing with infinity.*"

To help us open our vision, to get out of 'stuck' ways of seeing or experiencing things that limit our imagination, I asked the group to move around the room in two circles, one on the outside going clockwise, the other on the inside going anti-clockwise. We then merged the two circles, weaving in and out as we moved around, interacting with each person we met by exchanging wooden balls. We became very focused on the many tasks at hand; simultaneously giving and receiving balls with the correct hands, listening to the poem I was reciting and moving in time to its rhythm, figuring out who the next person was we would be meeting and whether to move to the left or right of them as we passed on to the next one. We started to get the exercise 'right' but in all our busy-ness were we really present to the lived moment?

So, I asked the group to do exactly the same exercise, but backwards—that is, to consciously lead with our backs and step into the unknown/unseen space behind us, not knowing what would happen or who we would meet. It was odd, even a bit unnerving, but strangely it seemed easier, more effortless and flowing. We couldn't see who was coming until they appeared before us! As Craig put it: "When we move backwards, it's as if I'm meeting new people! I'm suddenly much more aware of wondering whom I will encounter. My anticipation is heightened." "Exactly," I responded, "and yet these are the same people you saw when moving forwards." "Yes," said Craig, "It's as if I didn't see them properly until I had to walk differently and pay close attention! That makes me wonder how many other people I don't see around me in my life and work."

We tend to walk forwards through the world, knowing where we want to go, what we need to do, what we think we see. And yet it often seems that the more we think we know, the harder we try, the more the living moment and its promise of transformation slips from our grasp.

This is not irrelevant to our life in all too many parts of our world. It is not far-fetched to say that, at this time, we find ourselves standing at the edge of a chasm between 'knowing' how things *should* be, and not knowing how to get there. "Walking forwards" doesn't help on the edge of a chasm.

> Eurythmy comes from the Greek for 'harmonious motion.' A facilitator in social eurythmy has people move in ways that help sensitize them to their living form and embodied presence in space: how different spaces or movements express, or bring to one's attention, an awareness of themselves, of others, and of their environment that is otherwise not normally noticed or reflected upon.

Walking backwards, not in retreat but through a different landscape, just might. It's a leadership challenge. Going backwards rather than rushing over the cliff means going into the swirling, uncertain, ambiguous world of unknowing. That goes against every instinct of our habitual thinking, which so loves clarity and security. It can threaten our sense of self and personal identity. It takes courage to do it. But it's the generative route.

There are reasons to take it! As human beings we are our greatest resource. If we hold our certainties aside for a moment, allow that we don't see everything clearly, and pay attention as we move through life 'backwards' ready to be surprised, new possibilities emerge that we did not see at first. Forced into unfamiliarity and new encounters, we become aware not just of the world with which we are familiar, but also of the world of relationship and connectivity that seeing differently opens for us.

When walking backwards, conscious that we don't know what's coming, we discover that we *sense* our way into the unknown. The less we can see visually, the more our other senses are activated. This opening of our senses stills the chattering mind and stimulates an inner attitude of interest, of wondering what is going to happen, of being open to not knowing. It also sharpens our ability to perceive the whole before us, to find ourselves inside the moment ready to take the next step the situation is asking for.

Why call this 'playing with infinity'? Imagine walking a straight line, fixed, finite and clearly defined by you. You will move in crisp, clear, but bounded steps that don't allow much freedom for yourself, nor for the movement of others who bump up against you. There's not much room for change.

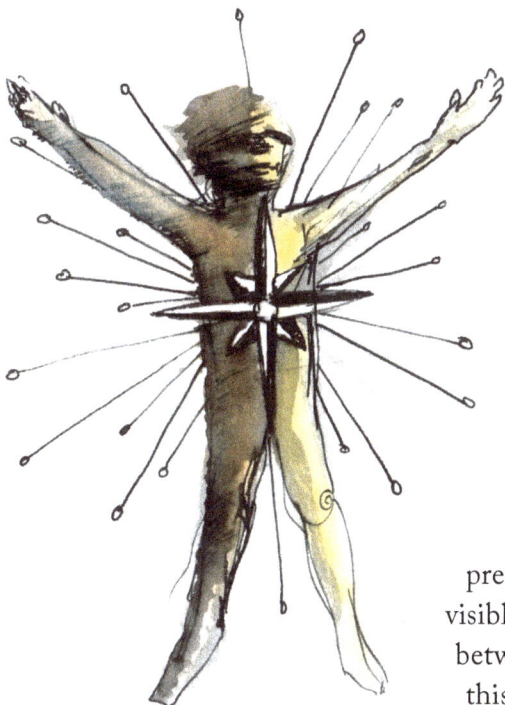

It often seems that the more we think we know, the harder we try, the more the living moment and its promise of transformation slips from our grasp

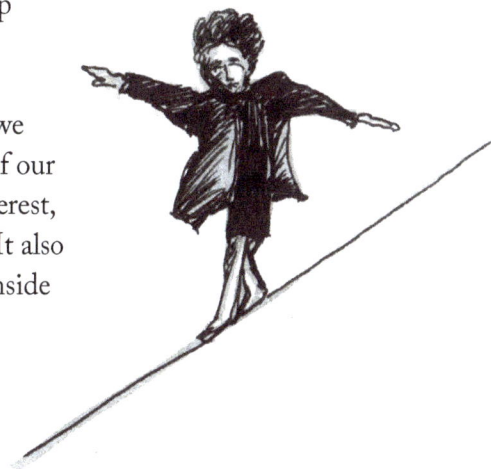

But a line is infinite; we don't have to define it as if nothing lies outside it. Instead we can step into a movement that is already living, whose origins and extent are unknown to us, bringing our own particular movement to its infinitude, making visible what is invisible but already there. We move and are moved by its flow, shifting and changing, going back and forth, creating a rhythm that starts to build and form a whole, which then carries us. So, we find ourselves inside a dynamic world of reciprocal movement and relationship whose very nature is possibility and transformation.

We have become very good at seeing, knowing and manipulating a limited way of viewing the world. The challenge is to develop and grow our capacity for the infinite, not as an abstract concept or something mystical, but as a generative, participatory, deeply embodied and very present way of seeing and being. We *are* the interface between the visible and the invisible, the finite and the infinite. We *are* the seeds between which new life comes into form. We only need wake up to this by sensing our way "backwards" into the living force, open and awake to what may come.

HOLDING SPACE AND TIME

Think of the difference being on a river or in a desert, working in a farmyard or an office block, walking through rolling hills or sitting in a prison cell, living in an affluent, lush suburb or in a settlement of tightly packed tin shacks.

What leadership means in each space we occupy will be shaped by that space. Spaces shape where we live and work, how free we are, how safe, how isolated or connected. Some spaces are highly constrained, preventing all but those who control them to do much; some are highly fluid, allowing people to move, to be free.

In the spaces we share with others, generative leaders actively embrace their presence by *holding the space* open in a way that allows for new energies and ideas to emerge from them. And by metaphorically (not literally!) *holding the person* in a way that allows their strengths to emerge.

Here's a story from Nomvula, one of our authors, that shows what this can mean.

People are going back and forth across the doorsill where the two worlds touch. The door is round and open. Don't go back to sleep.

EXPERIENCING EMPATHIC LISTENING AND A TRANSFORMATIVE PRESENCE

I'm in an intimate group of 12 people, in a remote and tranquil retreat to reflect on our leadership journeys. The woman leading us is a gentle soul. She helps us take ownership of our personal stories, make meaning of our lives. She's a quiet presence.

Not talking too much, she's attentive to our stories. She asks penetrating questions, wanting us to stand back from our individual stories so we can appreciate the bigger human story that connects us. 'Holding' us gently and lightly through her attentive presence, she reminds us we are called to be conscious leaders in our journeys of becoming, our search for meaning.

It strikes me how fully present she is to each person and the group, not imposing on us, a calming yet supportive presence. We can bring ourselves fully into the process, strong and weaker voices. Our resistances and biases find space in the conversations and are not forbidden.

The freedom is amazing. It invites honest conversation. It helps each of us travel to those places within ourselves that are sometimes difficult to reach. It is protected not by constraining boundaries but by respect for our dignity, our agency, our creative freedom, and our capacity to rise above ourselves. Instead of feeling bruised or violated, we are left feeling whole—feeling human. It "powers us up." It *brings something in me alive.*

I'm talking about a short-term experience of holding open the space and 'holding' the person as worthy of attention, respect, and care. But allowing people's voices to emerge, 'en-couraging' them to speak freely and openly, awakening something buried deep inside them, is key to any leadership worthy of the name. It evokes a moral responsibility to do right no matter the circumstances, to co-create a world that allows us all to be more human, individually and collectively.

Find more from Nomvula in *Barefoot Guide no. 4*, Chapter 3, pages 37-41, on "Finding your voice."

Short-term experiences of leadership that holds the space open are a good start. But if it is to change anything it will need duration, persistence, and determination, never giving up on the job of holding the space open. This, in turn, requires trust in the integrity and vision of those with whom one walks, as well as trust in the human capacity to live up to the highest of which we are capable.

In the 1960s Cesar Chavez's farm workers' movement not only changed the conditions of farm workers in the USA then, but it also inspired others subsequently, like Chicanos por la Causa (Chicanos for the Cause), to grow, flourish and claim the space Chavez and his compatriots had created. This fundamental commitment to generative leadership over the long march of human experience changes the world we live in for the better.

It's about space, physical and mental, and time in which to act, to express yourself, to have an opportunity to exercise your creativity and take some responsibility for doing so. Generative leadership means creating these kinds of opportunities for others, understanding what constrains it, and looking for new possibilities of making it happen to the benefit of all, including the institution or organization one serves (assuming, of course, that its goals are not in themselves harmful to others).

We often think of time in terms of deadlines (what a word!) and we measure progress in linear ways. We often assume that by the halfway mark of a project we should have achieved half the goals. When the work is creative and developmental, this is mechanical thinking that understands little of how the world works. Often, the most time-consuming work is relationship or trust building where progress cannot be measured on a score sheet, where indicators are simply invisible.

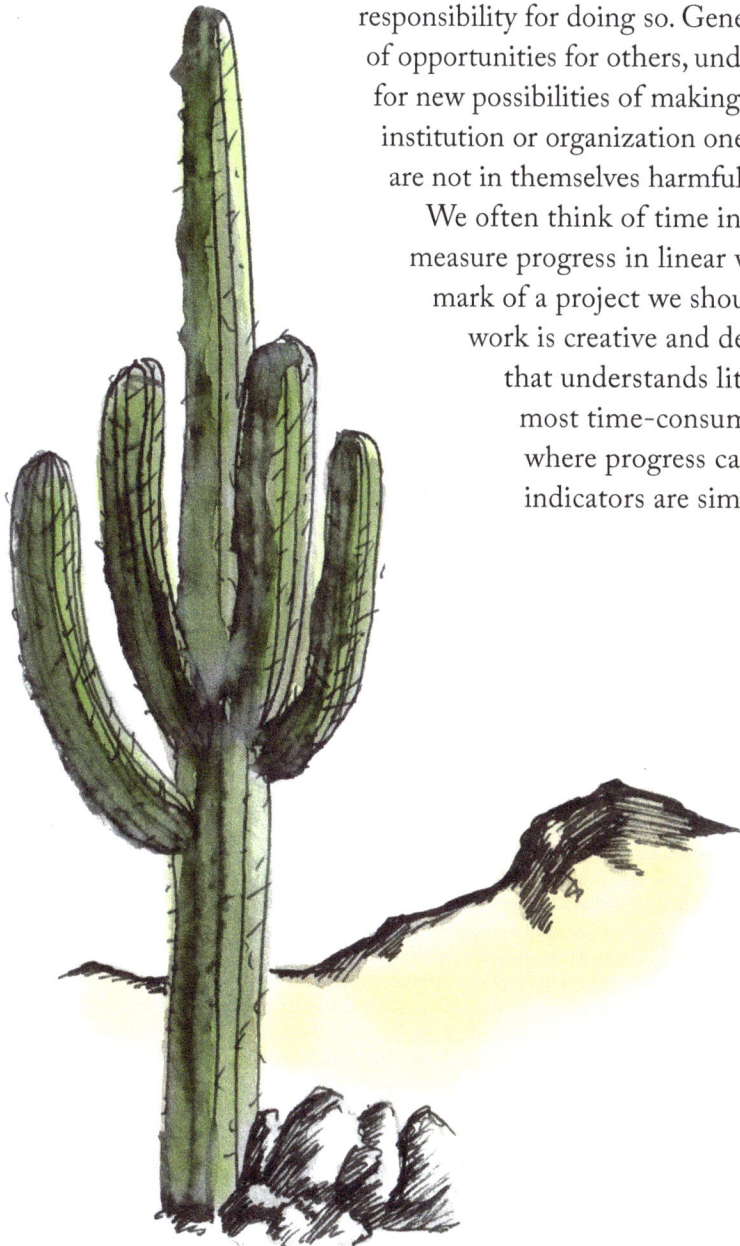

Often the most time-consuming work is relationship or trust building where progress cannot be measured on a score sheet, and indicators are simply invisible

Then, when the time is right, if there is respect and clarity and the will is unlocked, it is quite possible that the goals, and more, will be achieved quicker than expected.

Positional leaders who have authority in an organization or institution, can actually do a lot more in this way than they might imagine. Done well, these creative opportunities expand the organization's resources, the chances of innovation and robust problem solving.

Thinking creatively about the space and time you occupy with others and how you can maximize your own power or authority to open up space for others is one key to acting generatively as a leader.

BEING A PRESENCE

If time and space affects leadership, it's always in relation to being present with others. How does a generative leader think about that?

Taking a lead in anything means, whether we like it or not, that we will be judged by others, not just by what we do, but also by what kind of *presence* we have: how attentive we are, how comfortable with ourselves, how able we are to deal with tension and challenge and how much we are an integrity others can trust. Most people will quickly 'feel' or sense the kind of presence we are—someone of integrity, depth, wisdom, and care? Or merely someone with a separate agenda or interest of their own to serve. People will react accordingly.

The kind of presence we live out says a lot about our leadership, whatever formal authority or useful expertise we might have. It's often not about control or direction or even charisma.

What does 'presence' mean in this case? What is its relationship to generative leadership? How does it work? And what challenges does it raise in our practice as leaders?

'Being present' … to myself, to others, to group dynamics, and to the environment within which I find myself reflects a dynamic process of inner and outer gazing and engagement. It's about being *100%* attentive, both losing and sharing myself. It's supported by *valuing* others, encountering them with genuine awe, and entering their world through the enactment of *empathy*. It's being to *open* to myself, others and my context so that I am able to be sensitive, able genuinely to enter the worlds of others, to listen, hear and understand different ways of seeing and being.

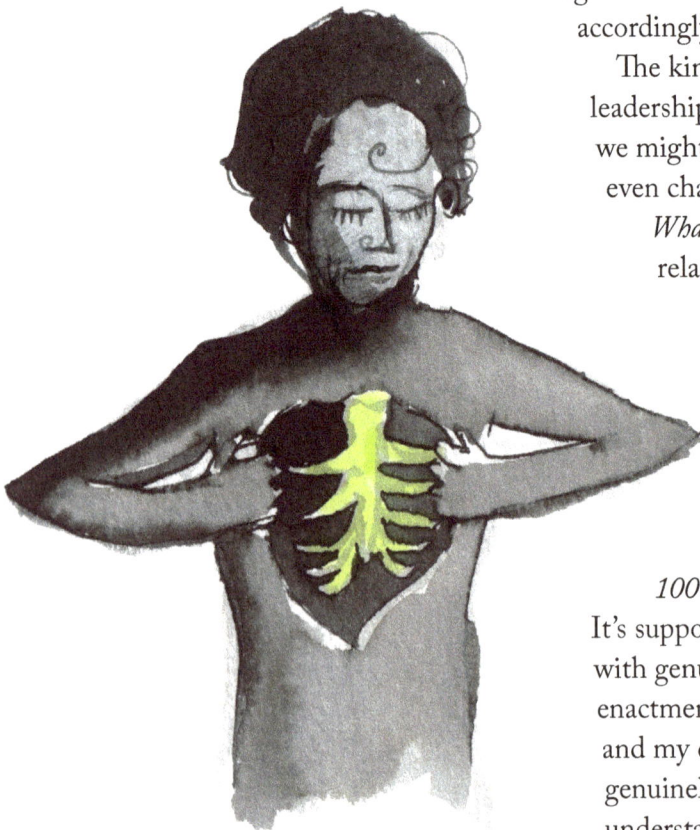

We can also call this *listening deeply* so that we can respond wisely to the needs of the moment. It's an idea explored in practice by Vietnamese Zen Buddhist peace activist Thich Nhat Hanh. It includes listening to and noting many things: the words that are spoken; the body's language of truth; the deep needs that are exposed; the interactions between people and the patterns these interactions create; and the local and broader conditions that are supporting or hindering healing and growth. Here listening is not passive; it is deeply active, engaging with self and others to check our understandings and posing questions that take us closer to understanding both dehumanizing and humanizing processes.

Presence demands what Eckhart Tolle describes as "an inner spaciousness that allows me to hold myself in a state of openness and conscious wakefulness." Then I am able to notice the natural forces of life within the system, "to watch what is happening and to witness the spaces between the thoughts and actions."

Authentic presence is not a planned strategy but a trustworthy way of being. Children quickly sense which it is, but those we find ourselves leading do too. Presence enables us to respond with wisdom, integrating our mind, heart and soul insights. It is presence that, in itself, creates healing, growth and therefore promotes life.

Being present helps us to 'read' the situation so that we can mobilize existing strengths and so nurture life-giving forces in the midst of life's difficult challenges. The mere act of listening with full attention and valuing the other with awe enables the other to 'be known', to feel accepted, validating the dignity of the other.

In essence, generative leadership begins with an acknowledgement of your own humanity that allows and invites the extraordinary humanity of others to be accompanied together in a common journey. The quality of your presence then flows into what you do and becomes transformative. Presence in this sense comes, we can say, from a place of stillness, the source of your creativity. More than being physically present, it's about becoming one with others and connecting in a way that enables you to create and hold a free space within which the inherent creative capacities of others can be unleashed. This allows you to identify the forces that block and undermine the agents of life, to see the broken relationships and connections that need re-weaving.

Where our leadership denies others their creative freedom, we place limitations on their inherent gifts and violate their dignity. In denying their human dignity we rob them of an opportunity to become co-creators of a more human world. Being present helps us to under-stand so that we can take a stand, calling on our own and others' agency, collectively exercising our inner power to act, and recognizing that we have the creative freedom to use this human power for good and bad, and so nurturing the moral responsibility for our actions that rejects dehumanization and promotes respect and the dignity of all.

Authentic presence is not a planned strategy but a trustworthy way of being

MARCELLINO'S STORY

My earliest recollection of what I consider generative leadership is when, as a young person of colour living in a township in the mid-Eighties in Apartheid South Africa, I was standing in a circle amongst my classmates listening to the telling of a violent incident in which a fellow classmate had been injured during a house burglary. We stood there with our hands in our pockets bragging about not being afraid to use kitchen knives to inflict grievous bodily harm on attackers.

As we went around the circle, describing our imagined scenarios of bravery, the images of violence escalated dramatically. Then one boy quietly admitted he wouldn't be able to hurt someone else so aggressively, no matter what the circumstances. He said he would do all he could to defend his family, but bloodshed was not something he was capable of.

We were shocked and stumbled over our responses. Just then the school bell rang to end our break, and we all walked to class deep in thought.

This was an extraordinary comment from an ordinary boy in a society where 'gangsterism' was the norm, physical violence a common occurrence, and manhood routinely questioned and having to be proven by fighting. It was a life-changing moment. His sincere and courageous response, in not wanting to be destructive, opposing the crowd's opinion, has guided me all my life when considering what it means to be human.

Our daily interactions, our differences in opinions and values inevitably lead to conflict or at least some disagreement. So how do we generate solutions without compromising our private beliefs and social values and without descending into conflict or violence?

This has been my work for a while now in SCRATCHMAPS, a project on Spiritual Capacities and Religious Assets for Transforming Community Health by Mobilizing Males for Peace and Safety. When I applied to be a community researcher in this organisation, I was not optimistic that I would get the position. The questions were very faith-based and as an openly gay person I doubted that I would be accepted. But I was! To me this was indeed a generative moment.

The community-based research team, with support from academics at South Africa's Medical Research Council (MRC) and the University of South Africa (UNISA), was composed of ten people, all non-academic community members ranging from their early twenties to late fifties. We had a wildly varying range of education and work experience, but our task was to help understand interpersonal violence among teenagers living in lower income neighbourhoods and to help develop, implement, and evaluate preventative interventions.

The local community, a poverty-riddled squatter camp, was asked to establish a project steering committee of elected local community elders who had final decision-making power over most project decisions. All had detailed access to information on money received and spent, printed on handouts available at quarterly open-door meetings. Over time, a community-based violent incident monitoring program was developed; regular community awareness campaign days were organized and a community-selected values-based Building Bridges youth mentorship program established. Throughout the process we received training in community-based participatory research methods. Our project initially focused on males but was soon expanded to include women and girls. Female mentors were necessary considering the dearth of willing males, and many young women were found to be just as complicit in incidences of interpersonal violence.

Before every team meeting, we "checked-in," briefly sharing what had recently happened to us and how it was affecting ourselves personally, allowing others a peek into our inner lives. This helped us see our common problems and built shared moments of empathy. It created an extraordinary environment for deepening our sense of ourselves as human, despite our adverse material conditions and the ramshackle house-church in which we met. We left sticky notes on project folders to make visible the organizers' thinking, we gently coerced the new intern to share an emotional truth at a work meeting to break down an emotional barrier, we shared insights and paid attention to each other's developing stories. Age was irrelevant as long as our knowledge was applicable and, more importantly, aimed in a socially constructive direction.

I imagine generative leadership as a co-operative effort for social justice helping under-served and under-privileged communities transform their circumstances, where individual action is invested with the expectation of direct communal benefit, and collective knowledge is applied to the societal arena to produce tangible results. Key to all this is helping people who are struggling through miscommunication and misdirection inside inefficient bureaucracies, to determine their own direction of growth and measures of development.

What becomes most important is constantly to show humility and a generosity of spirit in the most mundane, everyday interactions with people—a nonstop, gracious and sincere affirmation of the other person's best qualities, leveraging assets instead of lamenting lack. When we do this, we are opposing the kind of degenerate leadership in which people feel justified in exploiting opportunities to their advantage at the expense of others. False modesty can encourage us to belittle our individual inherent good, limiting the possibilities of our personal agency. Affirmation of who I am and what I can offer plants a seed, a blessing. It must be appreciated, acknowledged and nurtured to flower, to be consciously shared and regenerated, in myself and in others. That's the mode of being and doing that I would call generative leadership.

What becomes most important is constantly to show humility and a generosity of spirit in the most mundane, everyday interactions with people

LEADING LOVE

[Kirsten] What motivates our striving every day for the goals of social justice, equity, community well-being, health, an end to racism and oppression, and so on? I think it's love.

[Li Wei] Really? What do you mean by love?

[Kirsten] I mean nurturing—for myself, for others, for the world—a way of being in every moment that asks what love wants us to do in this situation, right now. Even in the midst of suffering, evil and ugliness.

[Leo] Is it just an emotional thing, about how you feel right now?

[Kirsten] Feelings change all the time, it can't be that. Love, I'm thinking, is not about my emotional state. I think it must reflect *an unrelenting commitment to our own well-being and to the well-being of others and our world*. Especially those least loved, those who are most vulnerable or marginalized, those who are usually 'not seen' by the powerful, the affluent and well-connected. Love demands justice and equity and peace.

[Li Wei] That's pretty demanding. But it raises difficult questions. What happens when the well-being of one group conflicts with that of another? What about people whose behaviour is abhorrent to us? How do we love oppressors and those who exploit others for their own gain?

Love also recognizes the ambiguity of evil in each of us and asks us to embrace the well-being of even those who hurt us

[Kirsten] Love as I mean it doesn't stop noticing, naming and confronting the evil present and active in our world. But love also recognizes the ambiguity of evil in each and every one of us, so it asks us to embrace the well-being of even those who hurt us. Of course, that's not easy. But it expands what we might be able to do together and how we might do it. And it's self-critical. It helps us admit our own complicities instead of taking ourselves to be right and everyone else to be wrong.

[Leo] How would you link that to generative leadership?

[Kirsten] I'd like to say it's about "leading love." Uncovering the deep connections, because our first aim is the well-being of the whole, to each other through which we will find the socially just way to live together or ways to be deeply creative in our quest for justice.

ABOUT "LEADING LOVE"

Often there are no obviously right answers. Love does not easily tell us what to do. We have to make hard choices in the midst of ambiguity and tensions. So, we yearn for leaders who tell us what to do. *Leading love* resists this seductive invitation for certainty. It keeps our reference point focused on what is most important as we navigate through complexity and chaos. It's what we follow when there is no good outcome or right choice. It helps us find the creative way through.

This requires a spiritual discipline, a kind of presence in the world that is hard to maintain. We have to hone our inner capacity to sit in the tensions and ambiguities with grace for others and ourselves. We have to have the courage to grieve, to lament, and to name the evil that wounds and strips people of their humanity. We have to foster that inner spark that finds the hope, peace and joy that is also always present in the midst of suffering.

It takes practice. For some it's found in religious ritual, for others in yoga or meditation. Some people run or hike. Some come together for intentional conversation. Whatever the practice, it's the work of the focused inner preparation needed to be able to see the options that love offers in those difficult, unclear situations.

This requires deep self-awareness and awakening to one's own vocation as a leader. Not the work of a special few who are smarter, better educated, more verbal and extroverted, it's a vocation we all share—a child, a worker, a teacher, a CEO, a homeless person. In relationships we participate in the leadership of others, and wisdom emerges in constant conversation with them.

This is completely different from the traditional understanding of what it means to lead. Its orientation is *hosting* versus heroic, creating space for the wisdom and work of the community to emerge, marked by a willingness to be changed and transformed in the process. It can be disrupting and messy. Walls may need to be broken down or built up, plants have to go to seed, or weeds have to be pulled out. It is not necessarily pretty. But when someone is making space or hosting well, you can feel it.

> *When we lead love, we are embracing the power of relationship across the spectrum of existence—from the microbe to the multiverse*

Love works. Look at any transformational process or quest for justice and fierce love is always at the heart of it. Greg Fricchione, a neurobiologist and psychiatrist, points out that evolution is not about the survival of the fittest. Living creatures, when faced with crisis or threat, are able to figure out or stumble into survival strategies that connect them constructively with other beings to be able to survive, adapt and develop. Even more so is this true of human beings. When we lead love, we are embracing the power of relationship across the spectrum of existence—from the microbe to the multiverse.

This relational impulse is foundational to our survival and well-being. Love counts on this.

LEADERSHIP AS HOSTING

Love is higher than opinion. If people love one another the most varied opinions can be reconciled—thus one of the most important tasks for humankind today and in the future is that we should learn to live together and understand one another. If this human fellowship is not achieved, all talk of development is empty.

- Rudolf Steiner –

One way to understand leadership is as hosting. Simple but profound, it's about creating the hospitable space that allows the wisdom and creativity of the community to emerge and for its members to connect and act. It assumes that the solutions already exist in people, that what matters is clearing away barriers and creating a structure within which people can think, build relationships, and start testing out what is wanting to emerge.

During our authors' Writeshop for this Barefoot Guide, we experienced what this means from our hosts at Mont Fleur Conference Venue. A wonderful location among the Fynbos of the Helderberg mountains near Stellenbosch, South Africa, it's not expensive or luxurious. It's meant to be very affordable and accessible. But it could match any place any of us had ever been to. Things got done when they needed to happen: space cleaned and tidied, food prepared and laid out, fires set just at the right time, and more … quietly, with no rushing around or anxiety or angry voices, no fanfare.

It was so elegant that we often didn't notice it, but we know how it feels: safe and pampered, cozy and intimate, surprised and delighted, engaged with nature and beauty

A sense of expansive possibility encased us because of how our hosts attended to us. Way beyond merely 'professional' (they were!), they gave us room to think and work—physical space, but especially emotional and spiritual space.

Kirsten, an author, wanted to find out more from the staff about how they create this kind of productive, rich environment. What she learned are practical principles of generative leadership.

Preparing with care. They educate themselves ahead of time: they know something about each person, what their special needs are, what the group's program and schedule is. They work out how to meet each person's needs, and already knew our names as we arrived.

Hosting with heart. Jo-Anne said about her hosting practice: "I do it all out of a sense of love. You have to love what you do, and I love serving people." We experienced this throughout from everyone. At our first dinner, a waiter Kirsten hadn't met or spoken to before brought her different food from everyone else's and set it in front of her without a word. How did he know without asking who she was and that she had an allergy to cater for?

Constantly observing and flexing. If we started trickling in for tea earlier than the printed schedule, the staff adjusted, setting out tea a little earlier next time. On a hike, our host Michael showed us some water blossoms that could be cooked in a stew. Next night, for dinner, we had water blossom stew. Coincidence?

Paying attention to detail. Did someone send their plate back with something uneaten? It was taken into account. "If we notice you don't like peppers," said Jo-Anne, "we make a note on a sheet in the kitchen and next time when we make your salad, we won't add peppers."

Adding small touches for pleasure. The first night, the bed was warm. An electric mattress pad had been put in and turned on as part of preparing the room for the evening. On colder evenings, a heater turned on after dinner had already warmed the room by the time we got there. And much more.

Communicating and working as a team. They help each other watch how guests are flowing so that they can move in and out unseen. One will ask another: Is it OK for me to go into the room to lay firewood now? Or they will alert each other that we are all at breakfast, so they can get into the rooms to freshen them up. They trust each other to do what needs to be done.

Being given responsibility and ownership. As Bridgette noted, "It is up to each staff person to do the work in their own area and to be accountable for it. It's not my job. They are the ones who are responsible, and they take responsibility without being pushed."

It's personal. When Jo-Anne was asked how they continually think, as they do, about bringing in nature and beauty into the physical space, she simply said: "It's my home too."

Practicing for a long time. Jo-Anne has been at Mont Fleur for 25 years. "She's part of the furniture, we are in her hands!" Eunice laughed. "I have been here for so long," Jo-Anne said. "that I know what is needed and how things should be done."

Allowing people to develop. Eunice began as a maid, then moved to waitress and now runs the front office. "She's quite an asset," Bridgette affirmed. "I can do all the jobs," Eunice said with pride, "There's room to grow here."

Forgiving and recognizing that conflict is part of relationships. "We have cat fights sometimes", Jo-Anne laughed. "We are people! But we are working through it. We still love each other."

Striving for excellence. Each day at a Getting Better Each Day (GBED) meeting they review how things are going to see what more they can do to host well. They elicit feedback from the guests and respond immediately to address any issues that are being raised.

This way of working is part of the fabric of their art of hosting, a culture that everyone lives in. What Mont Fleur offered is not servitude but active, practiced, skilled, intentional, and—yes—generative leadership.

THE RELUCTANT LEADER: PAUSING FOR ETHICAL LEADERSHIP TO THRIVE

Mosi one of our authors, speaks with a friend about how he understands 'reluctant leadership'.

[Mosi]   Imagine a leader who spends the first few months of the appointment to a top position saying: "I did not want this position. Neither did I actively seek it." And then providing leadership in ways that people recall with positive emotions long after he or she is gone.

[Ailia]   A reluctant leader? What is that? It sounds odd.

[Mosi]   I guess it does. Actually, it's all about an important insight into generative leadership.

[Ailia]   What kind of insight?

[Mosi]   That leadership is generative when it helps to open up and to grow the capabilities of others. It means going beyond any 'heroic' style, sustaining an ethos and process of inclusiveness, restraining one's own power, subverting (in oneself and others) leadership exercised for self-interest alone, and 'standing back' when the instinct is to lead and 'show you know better.'

The reluctant leader turns away from invitations to be given the mantle of a heroic problem solver or a victor over others

GENERATIVE QUALITIES OF A RELUCTANT LEADER

The reluctant leader turns away from invitations to be given the mantle of a heroic problem solver or a victor over others. The reluctant leader displays a spirit that disrupts the drive to leadership for self-promotion alone. In positions of formal authority, s/he tends to channel their leadership to advancing the creativity, freedom and dignity of those they lead. Hope is enhanced for people who now feel included and affirmed in their humanity.

What it means to be a 'reluctant leader' in practice can be seen in the story of Ashanut Okille, a young woman who lives and works in Uganda. She is such a leader. Her specific leadership qualities are reflected in the generative nature of her interaction with others, such as: 1) helping people to find energy and motivation in what they do for a living or in their own leadership of others; 2) helping individuals, organizations and communities make reflective connections to their past and find freedom in creating new paths of growth; 3) showing patience and forgiveness so that people may feel confident to learn and change.

Ashanut consciously applies such qualities in the organization she leads. In her own words: "I have kept my ambitions low. I temper my expectations of team members. I take stock of capacities available in the organization. I am happy with incremental progress. When we make visible small steps, however, we discuss what we can do to take it a notch further."[1]

GENERATIVE CONVERGENCE

The reluctant leader shuns positional leadership because of a fundamental suspicion that anointment is not always a gift but often an act of containment. The crown is a symbol of dominance—a model that boxes one into manipulative and controlling styles of leadership. Being trapped in the structures of hierarchical power is, to the reluctant leader, like a bird snared in the grass, branches of a tree or a poacher's hands.

The reluctant leader is not necessarily afraid of soaring to the loftiest heights of responsibility. Her leadership, however, comes to light mainly through being exposed to the agency of others, from whom she finds inspiration and energy.

The generative capacities of a reluctant leader are often influenced by individuals whose ethical actions touch others deeply—a parent who encourages a child to perform an act of justice, a teacher who refuses to brutalize children, or a community leader who makes great effort to re-organize social relations to leverage more equitable development.

Ashanut resigned from a well-paying job to start up a new initiative because in her leadership journey, she had internalized values that honour the experiences of people rather than negate or cancel any meaning they may discover for themselves. Such values have influenced how she uses power to leverage the creative freedom of others to emerge, in ways that her professional skills, tools and technique alone were not able to achieve.

Ashanut's resignation from the international organization she had worked for in Kampala was a conscious rejection of bureaucratic systems that, in their nature, do not generate people's capacities to imagine healthier futures nor promote their *agency* and *connections* to bring them about.

The unspoken wisdom in Ashanut's act is that leaders are ethical when their behaviours are leveraging hope for others. Keeping the world waiting is probably a necessary process for the reluctant leader, toward creating conditions where ethical leadership will thrive and have the appropriate impact.

Her choice to leave a bureaucratic organization that was offering greater personal benefits reveals her own *agency*, the capacity to enter freely and creatively into the world and work to change it with imagination and intentionality, to bring new possibility into being.

> *She uses power to leverage the creative freedom of others to emerge, in ways that her professional skills, tools and technique alone were not able to achieve*

THE INTUITIVE GUIDE

Anita, another of our authors, met up with Leo and Li Wei and shared her view on 'the intuitive guide'.

[Anita]   It's important to see that imagining generative leadership as acting in ways that push the river of life forward is not the same as aiming at accumulation, acclaim, or power. Rather than primarily about self-interest, it aims at enhancing our humanity and changing human systems for the better rather than demonstrating one's learnedness or power.

[Li Wei]   Yes, it would have to come from something deeper, purer, than mere ego. And all too often it's *ego* that drives the purely positional leader. As I experience it, the objective is control.

[Leo]   By contrast, the generative leaders I know, like a river, have a quiet but deep wisdom that often appears calm on the surface but is really tremendous strength underneath.

[Anita]   I would call this being more intuitive—coming from the right intention—which doesn't necessarily fit pre-determined plans or rigid structures.

[Li Wei]   I think that's why generative leaders often face enormous adversity. They are misunderstood by ego-driven systems, seen as insufficiently in-charge, too flexible, too open to turbulent currents.

[Anita]   Hmm, that's a good insight. Like the river, however, the generative leader does not let go of the objective, which is to reach the ocean. The river could form another tributary or meander slightly or widely or slow down momentarily, before it gains momentum again and crashes over precipices, but it will reach its destination.

[Leo]   Yes, so it is not deterred by adversity. Generative leaders are in for the long haul, they actually express a lifetime commitment toward achieving a humane goal.

The generative leader is not always visible

[Anita]   Another thing I find. The generative leader is not always visible. We commonly assume that we are either leaders or followers.

[Li Wei]   And this is not always true at all.

[Anita]   No, many 'ordinary' people with no leadership position or formal training, who do not regard themselves as leaders and often shun the leadership label, are exemplary. Many of them prefer being alone, pursuing solitary life-giving functions, like growing pumpkins on a roof in a food insecure neighbourhood or carving whistles out of wood, to give to children who have no toys.

[Leo]   It is not always the great and known ones like Mahatma Gandhi or Nelson Mandela. Mostly not. But it's always the one who is life-giving, like a river.

[Anita]   That's why I think of generative leaders as having a high level of consciousness or intuition, so I call them *Intuitive Guides*.

THE INTUITIVE GUIDE ...

The Intuitive Guide is like a river coursing through the land, taking along the silt and the sand and then quietly sliding past the boulders along its path.

The Intuitive Guide knows the landscape but is not the leader. Like the river, the intuitive guide serves.

The Intuitive Guide, like the river, has only the intention to nourish and this intention alone determines the actions of the intuitive guide. Those actions are often subtle and considered rather than planned and strategic and only dramatic when needed.

The Intuitive Guide, like the river, values life.

The Intuitive Guide, like the river, knows that freedom is fluidity and trust is a group activity. There is 'no me without them' and 'no them without me'.

The Intuitive Guide, like the river, gives freely and knows that we are all connected by our very breathing and the earth elements that make up our cells and our hearts and the life blood which courses through our veins.

The Intuitive Guide does not control.

The Intuitive Guide knows that all of life is energy. Air is energy and plants and trees are energy and belief and intention is energy.

The Intuitive Guide knows that living organisms are constantly reading the energy around them.

The Intuitive Guide's leadership holds the energy of its intention. Regardless of a leader's words, followers will take on the energy of the leader's intention. It happens at a subtle level. Intuitively, the river does not judge the piranha against the river otter. It simply takes it along to a common destination.

The Intuitive Guide's generative leadership is therefore almost always matched by intention. If we are unable to develop programmes and policies based on love for people, it will always be simple politics or mere social engineering experiments. The actions of love are generous and life giving. The river does not give more to the weeds than the bulrushes.

The Intuitive Guide is like ether, like consciousness, like a spiritual awakening that provides opportunity for potential to flourish. S/he removes blockages, creates opportunity and holds the privileged accountable. However skilled and capable people at the helm, love for people is the plaster that builds.

The Intuitive Guide knows that generosity replicates itself. Generosity, more than training, brings life to dead places.

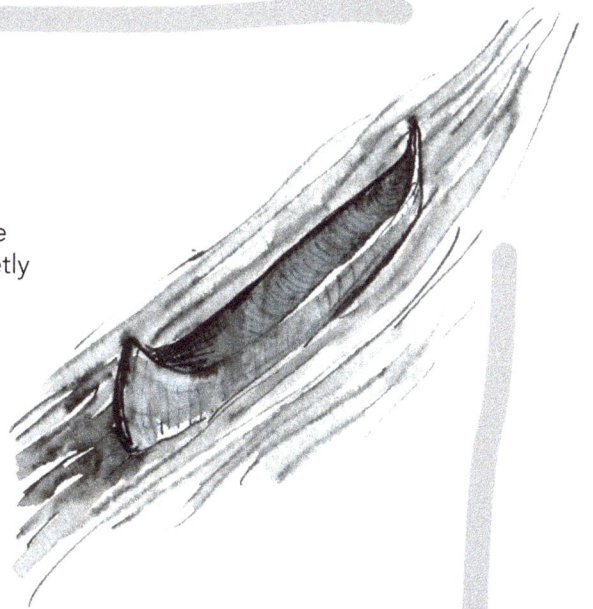

[Leo] There are lots of interesting thoughts and ideas in this chapter, but I worry that it could be understood as focusing too much on the individual leader as some kind of 'guru' or 'special person.' I mean, even a highly sophisticated group or community facilitator often appears simply as another kind of positional leader, someone who is the expert in what they do and that others assume they cannot do without lots of training and learning, and who is seen as the one who will determine things.

[Anita] Good point. Most of the authors of this Barefoot Guide would be in that kind of position. You are pointing to our shadow side. That makes it important to read this chapter—actually, the whole book—while being fully aware of our shadow side. It can easily work against what we understand as generative leadership.

[Leo] Yeah, we don't want that.

[Li Wei] There's no simplistic answer to this challenge. At least one way of dealing with it, which should be as transparent as possible, is to talk about the DNA of the group and not just the individual. If we want to sustain generative leadership we must see it in promoting a 'culture of leadership' rather than in the qualities or character of a particular leader.

[Anita] Agreed. But at the same time, this must not take away the responsibility each of us has for our life and work in the world. Each of us—no matter who we are and whether or not we are in a so-called position of leadership or authority—has the capacity, simply by virtue of 'being (and becoming) human,' to take on the culture of leadership we describe as generative.

If we want to sustain generative leadership we must see it in promoting a 'culture of leadership' rather than in the qualities or character of a particular leader

CHAPTER 6

FLOWING FORWARD

"Possibility above actuality"

A river, no matter how beautiful, does not exist only for itself. The forces of life flow with it, complex cycles turning and unfolding, from the rain falling and gathering in springs and rivulets that converge, finding strength and fullness before emptying into the boundless ocean. Even the little river in Cape Town that caught our imagination early in our writing collects itself from the watershed on the eastern side of Table Mountain, finds its way nine or ten kilometers toward the waters of Table Bay and the Atlantic, and loses itself in the great mingling of water from all rivers and oceans, rising again with sun and wind to form clouds, once more to rain.

Leadership is like that. It finds its long perspective beyond day-to-day management in the great purposes that connect the smallest elements of life, making sense of the cycle of life from past to present to future, as future becomes present and present becomes past. Our best work finds its purpose in locating our lives as integral with the whole. Our short lives are not small when joined to the great story unfolding beyond our knowing.

We've learned some river wisdom in writing, and we gain more as it flows to its end, ready for new beginnings. You will be at very different stages of your experience and learning, your flow. We do not say to you: "Ride the same current we have found for ourselves." We do not simply want you to imitate the approach and language we find useful. Rather, we hope you will be inspired to live in your own moment, by your own account, finding your own way to be integral with your time and place and whatever they may offer. Nonetheless, we have hope that, just as rivers join at the ocean, there is confluence as we find our different ways to our shared humanity.

And that's it. Finding our shared humanity. Not just as an idea, but in our doing. We live in times of unparalleled wealth and scientific innovation but also—for the masses of marginalized and oppressed human beings on all continents—of inexcusable suffering and degradation. This is our greatest challenge, the real test of whether we can indeed call ourselves generative leaders.

So, in this last chapter, we bring a personal story that explores dimensions of that challenge, some concepts and practical ideas "for change-makers," and a short commentary on the difference between a vision of death and one of life. We end the chapter, and this book, by focusing on exactly that last issue—the bold but vital task of "working with life."

People who know the rules, know what is possible and impossible. They do go beyond the rules to test the bounds of the possible. You can. And if you don't know it's impossible, it's easier to do[1]

OUT OF SOUTH AFRICA,
A PERSONAL TALE

South Africa, a quarter century after Apartheid's formal end, is amongst the most unequal countries in the world and still deeply segregated—most black people are still poor and most white people are well-off. Its cities have no real plans to build integrated neighbourhoods and residential segregation continues on the basis of income differentials, still a mirror of the Apartheid past. This sheer inequality and its racial bias continues to do deep long-term harm to society as a whole. It is inconceivable for generative leadership not to confront such realities—and not just in South Africa!

What might it mean to confront these realities, these 'actualities,' and to open up and build on the new possibilities that lie hidden within them? Here's one person's story, Horst's story, of an attempt to figure that out in relation to the troubled history of his own family.

It is inconceivable that generative leadership does not confront the realities of inequality and discrimination

HORST'S STORY

Horst Kleinschmidt was an Anti-Apartheid activist and student leader detained under Apartheid laws and forced into exile in Europe for 15 years. In exile he led the International Defence and Aid Fund for Southern Africa (IDAF) that supported political prisoners and their families and was part of the organizing committee of the "Release Mandela" International Tribute Concerts at Wembley Stadium, London, televised in 67 countries to an audience of 600 million. A recipient of the Austrian Bruno Kreisky prize for Services to Human Rights (1991), he was also knighted in 1999 by the King of Sweden with the Order of the Polar Star (First Class) for his role in aiding political detainees and prisoners in Southern Africa. He returned to the newly democratic South Africa in 1994 to work on environmental and human rights.

Horst comes from a family of missionaries, the earliest of whom arrived at the Cape in 1811. In 1814, one of his fore-fathers, Missionary Hinrich Schmelen, married his catechist, a woman of indigenous Khoi-khoi origin, and they lived in Komaggas, Northern Cape. Horst discovered this closely kept "family secret" of a 'mixed marriage' in 2012. He also learned that members on the other, 'white' side of his family had supported the Nazi regime in Germany. Since then he has sought to reunite both his white and 'coloured' families. This is his story.

CONFRONTING MY HISTORY

"Research into my family interested me because I sensed a secret the family wanted to keep until no-one could remember it. I knew it had to do with race, but initially I did not connect our family history to the broader race-based society we lived and continue to live in. It took time for me to escape the cocoon of race-based thinking. The zig-zag journey led up many blind alleys and it still continues. In 2012, I was able to verify that my great, great, great grandmother was a native African Khoi woman, and I met the other side of my family for the first time.

For me to claim Khoi ancestry might sound like I simply want to escape my 'white' family's cursed colonial legacy and ethos. To claim that ancestry may even be subliminal racism – a way of saying: "See, I'm not really white, and I'm not as racist as you might think I am." I want to be aware of that. Racism is one important tool to assert one's class over others. Rejection of the other follows.

So, I use my family example, available to me by coincidence, as a means to challenge the concept of race as a way to assert social position in a social hierarchy that always places white people at the top. My public claim of a Khoi ancestor is to counter and destroy the belief in the prowess of whiteness, first within my own family but, more importantly, to encourage those many other white people who are not really 'white' to find out – and once they have found out, to note that nothing is the matter with them; they are just as ordinary as any other human being. Such a journey liberates us from the prison in our mind, one that imposes such a terrible burden on us all.

I (or we) might think or feel we are not racist, but we come from a racist past and carry its remnants in us. Race is enmeshed in our language, in our social values, and in our judgements. Maybe in that nagging impulse we cannot suppress that we are materially better off because 'we are smarter', maybe in countless other thought processes that are not overtly expressed but appear at the sub-liminal level, where it never needs to be admitted or confronted. Fear and lack of knowledge about the 'other' explains one part of race obsession.

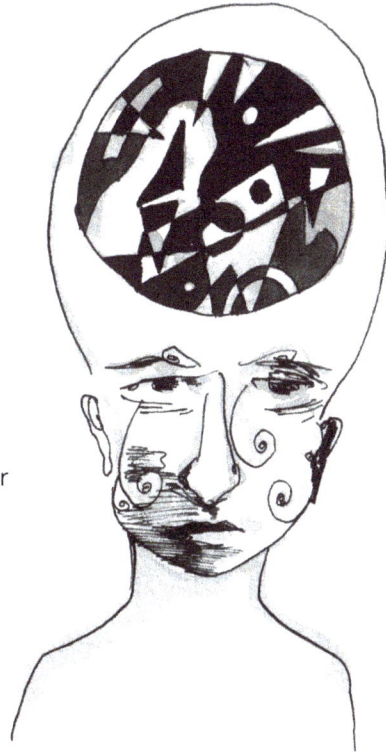

White or dominant class acceptance mostly requires that the other becomes 'like me,' that is, accepts my social norms and values. But racism has another leg it stands on: Class. It rests on material inequality and the eternal scramble to assert material well-being over others.

Nelson Mandela was right when he asserted that racism does not come naturally; it is taught! And if it is taught it can be untaught. What he failed to say, why his wisdom falls short, is that inequality, the gap between rich and poor, the scramble for riches, is the material basis for racism. In the end, our South African predicament of overcoming apartheid is only truly realized when the material base between all its people is, to whatever extent possible, equivalent.

Should we then be promoting a negotiated transfer of wealth? Should the rich be willing to talk about it? How can we support hopeful change and not just wait until chaotic change engulfs us all? Is my assertion ahistorical? There are means to speak to our material inequality. Restitution requires both dealing with the racism in our daily conduct and dealing with material inequality. Our status as one of the most unequal societies, twenty-five years after majority rule in South Africa, is unsustainable and it will destroy us. It requires bolder proposals than those advocated by the good people on both sides of our social divide.

So, these are the lessons I draw:

Researching and writing about my family history serves as a way to de-racialise the race mythology in remnants of our family and wider society. I want to debate and debunk these myths. I want to confront my past, so it may encourage others to do this in their families. Coming from the dominant and advantaged side of my 'mixed' family, generative leadership places demands on my approach.

Vestiges of racism probably lurk in all of us, whether we think we have liberated ourselves or believe racism was never part of us. To ultimately 'clean' ourselves of all racial thinking is unlikely to happen, at least in our generation. What then? The chance we have of an equal society is to learn to know of the prejudice that lurks inside of me, possibly all of us 'whites', to remind me (and us) again and again to recognize when my thought or action relies on prejudice or rejection of the 'other'. Knowing the demon means I can challenge it.

To really get to understand 'white privilege' and how it has and is paving the way for white people to be who they are and have what they have.

Racism ultimately relies on material inequality. To fight the scourge of racism we also need to struggle against material inequality, especially that which is handed down from Apartheid to those with continuing privilege today.

In all of this, in South Africa, I specifically have to be the generative leader we speak of in this book."

THE NOBILITY WE ARE

Here's an interview with Somava Saha, who knows what it means to try to live as a generative leader in large organizations and institutions whose mission is to make a difference in the world, yet whose influential channels of power and command can make it extremely challenging to act in a way that is generative. Somava heads up the 100 Million Healthier Lives initiative, convened by the Institute for Health Improvement in Boston, an organization whose impact is felt around the world. 100 Million Healthier Lives intentionally seeks to distribute power by trusting, connecting, and growing the leadership of other people, organizations and communities who collectively generate the solutions needed to improve health, well-being and equity.

> *She could see abundance where others would have only seen what was missing*

Gary: So how'd you become you?

Somava: I'd start with conversations on the veranda with my mom. I grew up in Calcutta. My family made about $10 a month. We lost electricity every night, but we were housed. Every night my mom, a math teacher, would stand on the veranda and ask me lots of math problems (I got good at math!). But she would also ask me to look at the world around me, at how many people ... it turns out millions ... had so much less than we did. She would invite me to consider how many gifts and talents I could use to make a difference. It's our job to use them to create a better world for all.

Gary: This was not imaginary abundance. She wasn't making it up. She could see abundance where others would have only seen what was missing.

Somava: Right. And she taught me at an early age to see that in others. Even those sleeping on the streets, the poor, not as poor, but actually as an ocean of trapped and untapped human potential, of community, of generativity.

Gary: What you're describing is a little bit more radical, yet humble, than just generative leadership. It's liberating.

Somava: Yes. Actually trusting in the abundance. A lot of things in my life have reinforced this. Coming to the USA, I moved from India to Indiana, which literally translates to "not India"—and it wasn't. I learned what it meant to feel really different, which could be incredibly difficult. But at no point did my mom stop feeding me with a narrative of possibility.

Gary: Say more about what that meant in reality.

Somava: My mom did not know how to navigate things in the USA, what direction I should take. So she taught me to deal with uncertainty and ambiguity—to be very resourceful in figuring out how you get from place A to place B, and to trust that it was possible. The question was never the "what," it was always the "how."

In India she would say, "When you grow up, you should try to be great." And I'd go check out books, try to learn what that meant. I laugh at myself because I was rather earnest as a kid. It wasn't her way of protecting me, it was her belief in what was possible—not the award or recognition, but of doing something that makes a difference for the better in the world. That felt much more like a North Star.

Gary: And once you were in the USA?

Somava: In college at Harvard I saw people sleeping on the streets again. I had no idea why they were there. In India I understood it. There they were poor, they'd come from villages. But why in the wealthiest country in the world, outside the wealthiest university in the world? When people on the street would ask for change, I said, "Would you have a meal with me?" and asked to listen to their story. And that gave me a sense of what was happening here—social and spiritual poverty along with resource or structural poverty, a poverty of stigma and social isolation that made things so much worse.

Gary: What helped you deal with this?

Somava: I became a Bahá'í. That's a really big part. It gave me a framework and tools for thinking about how you take these things because it starts with some core assumptions about how you create change. You recognize people as intrinsically noble, that education is not just about learning or skills but about uncovering the gems already in each person. We're interconnected as a human family so it isn't about me being superior and doing something for you because you are less or deficient.
It's about walking alongside one another, where others' gifts and potential are unleashed, which contributes to my own development. We don't have all the pieces of the puzzle needed for the healing of the world. Everyone has something that is needed for the healing of the world. Our job has to be to create the conditions for that contribution, that liberation, to be realized.

Gary: What about institutions, do you think of them as noble too?

Somava: They can choose to create the conditions that unleash nobility. In my experience of building a system of shared learning in partnership with those who are most affected, this means being humble enough to ask: does this work? To learn from one another, to build more together than you ever could have alone. To have the courage to try things because you're not afraid to fail, and to abandon what doesn't work.
I've learned this watching people in the Rupununi region in Guyana, the second poorest region in the second poorest country in the Western Hemisphere, who utterly transformed their outcomes. I've seen it across our 100 Million Healthier Lives communities as they take on challenges they never would have been able to solve if they hadn't been courageous and in relationship with people who are most affected. I've seen it with homeless women right here in Skid Row; they took a Diabetes Prevention Program, adapted it to be what was really needed for people.

We can choose to create the conditions that unleash nobility

It transformed not just the lives of the women but, over time, also of system leaders and their institutions who were reconnected back to their mission, back to their nobility.

Embedded in it all is an invitation and an opportunity to grow the number of people who are thinking and acting in a different way that helps them reclaim their nobility. This creates abundance. It's more than the sum of any one of those strategies or any one of those organizations. It's the possibility of what can be created when those pieces of the puzzle come together. Knowing that no one of us is enough.

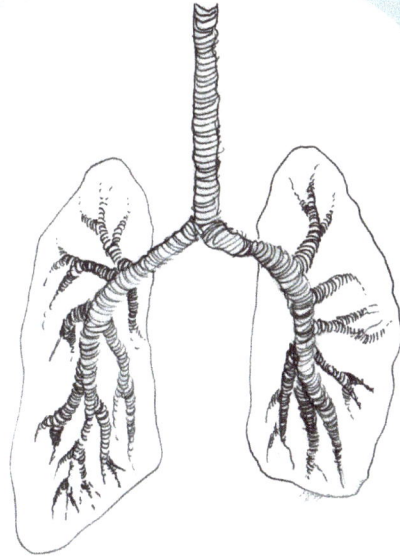

Gary: Few people have been as immersed as you in big institutions with profound financial and science challenges and accountable community dynamics. You've lived inside the machine. How do you change it?

Somava: Like poking holes, the concrete to allow a river come back to life, I create spaces in the machine that allow human spirit to emerge. This creates the conditions for not just life for the people, but a reclaiming of the mission of the institution. That's what happened at Cambridge Health Alliance. One hole was changing the finances, but a bigger hole was capturing the imagination of the people in the organization, inviting them to create the change that would build an organization they would be proud of. Making its mission of improving the health and wellbeing of its community front and center again by inviting people to partner with patients, with communities, to do whatever was needed to do that. It worked. It's not complicated, actually. When you get close to the people who most need it and you listen to what creates wholeness in their lives, you pay attention to how you can change the system to enable that wholeness.

Gary: So it's a breaking of the old containers.

Somava: And old mindsets. That's probably the most concrete container preventing new possibilities.

Gary: You're a scientist, and you're an institutional leader. How do you do this generative work in such a cynical time?

Somava: Well, first stay connected with who we're doing this for and why. Ground yourself in communities, make sure people with lived experience are part of the part of the conversation, not sideways, but at its heart. Pay attention to what they bring, not as recipients, but really as leaders in the process. The drama up among people who are positioning for power actually can't compete with the power of who human beings are with one another. You don't fight a battle over facts with other facts; you battle it with love and relationship, with people knowing one another.

Gary: Tell me a little bit about tools of generative work, the things to work with that fit this almost poetic language.

Somava: We talk about the Community of Solution Skills. It's about seeing communities as having trapped and untapped potential that can be liberated. And about moving from a place of fear of failure to a space of learning, about having the courage to dream of what real change could look like and then to pursue it. About how the community creates abundance, how they see the assets in their organizations or relationships, how they plan for sustainability, and how they work not just with one another but with those most effected by inequity. These are skills of co-design, but also of leading from the heart, leading from within.

Gary: For example?

Somava: Well, your ability to reflect, to challenge yourself, to be connected with your own history, to reclaim it and own it and understand how it led you to become who you are. Building relationships through knowing one another's stories. Understanding the organizational stories and the community stories and history. Recognizing what you could do together that you couldn't do alone. Grounding it in real lives getting better, holding ourselves accountable for that, and keeping this as your focus. This isn't some theoretical thing on a page. It's about understanding the root causes of inequities, how they got created, what it means to dismantle the system, leading for sustainability, and doing so at scale. Changing the policies, the environment, but also growing the change process so that more and more people can begin to think like this. Then connecting them so they can see how, together, they're engaging in much larger scales of change through their relationships with one another. It's a way of thinking about the world differently. We don't have to come up with all the answers. We need to step back and create the right spaces, along with many others, to hold the whole so that those connections can be made. Like any mom who has to let their child go because she trusts and believes in who they are, this is crucial.

Gary: That's really counterintuitive for a role called "leader." If you are no longer the one who has to do the fixing, that leaves a big gap in many leaders minds. What's their value now?

Somava: I now get to be part of a community of change-makers, right? In trusting the potential and agency of the community, I am trusted too. That's mature leadership, that's what allows me as a leader to blend my identity with what matters to the community. And that's a profound step in living for a better world.

PRACTICES FOR CHANGE-MAKERS

Horst's and Somava's stories tell us about some of the most difficult but nonetheless crucial challenges we face in our world. These situations can overwhelm us. But that doesn't necessarily mean it is time to give up. It means we need to enter into a process of discernment, usually with others, who can help us see and understand the picture more clearly to help us make decisions that matter.

Here are some concepts and practices that may be particularly relevant and helpful at these times:

- *"Drill holes to find the river - critical hope"* – Critical hope demands a committed and active struggle to create social change despite the evidence of its difficulty. It does not ignore the reality of toxic social environments, but persists in its face, acting with courage like "roses that grow from concrete" (Tupac Shakur, as quoted by Duncan Andrade, 2009).

- *"Look into the depths - deep discernment"* – holding the tensions we face in life invites us in life-giving ways to embrace paradox. At the intersection of hurt and hope, of faith and fear, there is a place which is life-giving even as, like a double-edged sword, it may threaten to take life. To see this requires practices that help us discern where we are on the journey and that, with others, helps ground us.

- *"Find the clear pools - clearness of council"* – a simple but powerful and potentially liberating process used at critical times where one invites two or three other people to ask deeper and deeper levels of open, honest questions (questions they could not know the answer to), reflecting back what was answered without any advice but in order to listen.

- *"Tumble with the rapids - failing forward"* – recognizing that, although the path to effective change *will* be strewn with failure, the richest learning for oneself and others comes from failure (actually, science at its best works this way as well!). Effective change often means to learn to fail fast, learn quickly and move forward. Children know this and are not afraid to fail. Imagine a one-year-old who was too afraid to fail to walk!

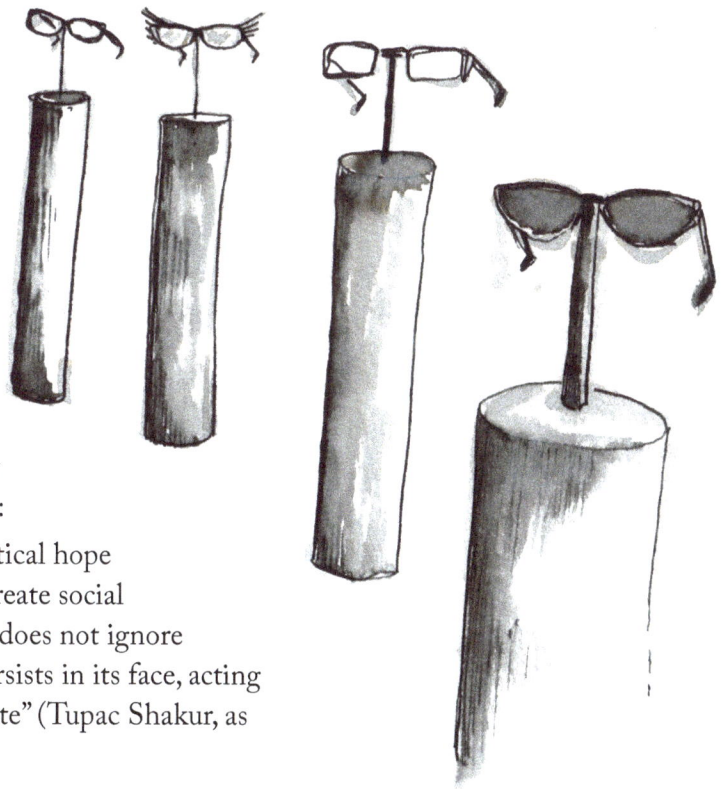

- *"Embrace failure"* – One key element of failing forward, however, is to be willing to embrace failure, not just individually but socially and culturally, to recognize and honour it rather than to punish it even in subtle ways and to welcome it as a friend when it arrives. It also brings with it a great gift—it creates safety and space for growth for oneself and others.

- *"Be together against the flow"* – It is crucial for change agents to have others together with them as they take on difficult inner and outer questions. The practice of leading together helps us to not be alone in these choices. It allows us to reflect on a situation together, knowing that we are not alone, seeing when it is a time to hold on and dig deep—and when it is a time to let go.

- *"Shake the dust from your feet – letting go"* – In the Baha'i tradition if one possesses knowledge it must be offered to others as we would "a jewel to a king." If it is not accepted, we are invited to "shake the dust from [our] feet" and move on, knowing that the value of the jewel is no less. Learning to let go and knowing that it is okay is one of the most difficult challenges that change agents face.

Be willing to embrace failure, be willing to let go when it's necessary

- *"Honour the riverbanks - being the hollow reed"* – One of the most helpful things for me is to remember that I am part of a whole of creating change—not instrumental within it. A Baha'i prayer that reminds me of this is about an instrument: "Lord, make me a hollow reed, from which the pith of self hath been blown, that I may become a clear channel, through which Thy love might flow unto others." Remembering that my role is to be the reed, not the light—that I am but one of many, many reeds, helps me to let go and be part of what is happening in the world, to be in the flow rather than trying to drive the flow.

  - *"Gather by the river - caring for oneself"* – Often change agents care for everyone else and the world around them and fail to care for themselves. This can look different for different people. Whatever it is for you, without giving into egoism, it's vital to keep one's own sense of balance, of own well-being without guilt, of groundedness, of discernment, of courage, of critical hope, of connectedness with the whole.

A DIFFERENT VISION: "FULLNESS OF LIFE"

(blog by Stephen Brown, posted June 3, 2017 by Phil Tunis)

"If my actions are to make a difference to the future, don't I need a different vision than the one that seems to dominate now?" asked Jürgen Moltmann, a Christian theologian famous for his *Theology of Hope*, on the recent 500th anniversary of what we call the Protestant Reformation, a movement that in part rose up against the economic exploitation and political subjugation of the German people in the 1600s.

In this time of exploitation and subjugation, Moltmann is thinking of how new scientific and technological possibilities can be used for the hurt, harm or death of humanity. This comes from what he calls the "gods of death": racism, war, nationalism, an economic system that produces ever greater inequality among people, and the terror from below of "suicidal mass murderers" motivated by a "religion of death." These realities threaten us as individuals, groups and as a whole. Sometimes they seem so dominant that we don't know where to turn. It feels as if it is just *the way things are* and there's not much to be done about it.

We act for a different future knowing that possibility is above actuality

But for Moltmann they are not the end of the story, they don't determine everything. A different vision is possible, a vision of what he calls the "fullness of life." It's one that looks for the life that breaks free despite the forces of death. Against being caught up in the way things actually are, he says, "Anyone who trusts the future sees the world according to its potential." It's full of real possibilities, in the present, that bring life rather than death.

He is not naïvely optimistic: the "gods of death" don't simply disappear, but neither are they necessarily triumphant. "The cry for justice," he said, "always comes too late, when violence and wrongdoing make the life of vulnerable people difficult; but it has to come. We will therefore become seekers of possibilities of life and justice and will avoid the recognizable options of death and annihilation." What matters is that our *actions for justice are life-giving*. This, for him, is what it means to speak of "the confession of the living God."

You don't need to share Moltmann's particular religious tradition at all to see here what matters for exercising generative leadership: a vision of life rather than death as determining; or, put differently, that we act for a different future knowing that possibility is above actuality.

RADICAL INCLUSION

More than ever, today's leaders compete for the trust and confidence of those they lead. So say Martin Dempsey and Ori Brafman in their book, *Radical Inclusion*,[2] on how leadership needs to change dramatically. They see major challenges.

One is the speed and accessibility of information. This creates what they call "digital echoes" that make facts vulnerable and easily manufactured. Whether this is deliberate or by default, it erodes trust between leader and follower. The nature of power is also changing in ways that mean it can't be measured by control alone. Control is seductive but it's no longer likely, if it ever was, to produce optimum, affordable, sustainable solutions.

So, they say, leaders today must, first, "relinquish" and share control to build and preserve power. Second, fear of losing control in our fast-paced, complex, highly scrutinized environment is pushing us toward exclusion and this, they believe, is exactly the wrong direction. Instead we need an instinct for "radical inclusion," and it's urgent.

Lots here matches what we say in this Barefoot Guide: the significance of earning and sustaining trust; that control is the wrong way to go; the error of excluding others as a means of preserving ourselves; and the urgency of inclusion. We would add: It is into the future that we must direct ourselves, flowing forward, knowing we control the future less than we control a river's flow. We can build safeguards to give us some stability and confidence for the future but, like a canalized river, they are no guarantee that human life will thrive, never mind the world upon which we depend.

Here's the vital point: The present is filled with innumerable possibilities! *Which* possibilities we see and choose to pursue is crucial. *We are capable* intentionally of aiming at generative rather than degenerative possibilities.

That's a mark of what it means to be and become human. However much we struggle with our own limits or failures, however much others or circumstances may appear to derail us, it is possible to live up to the highest of which we are capable as human beings. However seldom we reach those heights—most of us are not heroes, after all! —it's more than enough to know we can … and to live out of that knowledge. It happens in history, we thrill when it happens, and we can be part of it happening. The poets know this too, and here's one who has said it as well as any …

After Tischbein by JRC

THE HOLY LONGING

JOHANN WOLFGANG VON GOETHE

Tell a wise person or else keep silent

For the massman will mock it right away.

I praise what is truly alive

And what longs to be burned to death.

In the calm waters of the love nights

Where you were begotten,

Where you have begotten,

A strange feeling comes over you

When you see the silent candle burning.

Now you are no longer caught in this obsession with darkness

And a desire for higher lovemaking sweeps you upward.

Distance does not make you falter.

And now, arriving in magic, flying

and finally, insane for the light

You are the butterfly.

And you are gone.

And so long as you haven't experienced this,

To die and so to grow,

You are only a troubled guest on a dark earth.

WORKING WITH LIFE

In this Guide, you'll notice missed opportunities as well as what's worth keeping afloat. We've worked hard to lay out our best mind and spirit, to share the vital clues that give us hope, and the uneasy warnings about what we find to be untrue. Hear it as encouragement not to waste a moment of your time in the flow of life given to you and those around you.

It's this simple: The strength of generative leadership lies in the confidence that we are *working with life*. Not just *for* life. Far less just fighting those things that might threaten it but as co-workers with the most basic driving force of all creation. Life works, maybe the only thing that works over time.

From this angle, generative leadership is easier, more natural. Not worrying overly about what we can and can't control, it sees that the flow of life carries us rather like a river. Life can't be denied, channeled in concrete, or even dammed for a season. It will flow and find the sea.

Life may be the only thing that works over time

Our work is not without sweat, even danger. A glacier moves with gravity and grows with the snow, and if it is too warm it will melt and flood. But we have choices. If you love your children, the planet and the cities near the sea, you will not want to add to the melting with foolish and needlessly wasteful choices. Working with life tells you what to avoid, just as it tells you how to participate in the co-emergence.

We may be blocked by a temporary but precarious array of forces and contraptions that hold back mercy and justice and life. This may be daunting, dangerous and arrogant— but not worthy of fear. It's not just our little programs against death, it's life against death.

That's a fair fight, all any human can ask for. Leadership with life is a choice to be part of the beating heart of ongoing creation.

Tony Atala, a daring researcher at Wake Forest University who does such seemingly miraculous things as growing new body parts, knows that if you give a few unrelated heart cells a trellis and friendly medium to grow, they will find each other. They will beat together, not at Tony's command, but because they want to. Does Tony think it might it be natural for us humans to find each other, a common cause, and a way to be together so that we might be the organ the body politic needs in order to live? Of course, he said, but unlike organs, humans need some facilitation, encouragement to remember their true character, some leadership—not to do the leader's will, but to find their own essential and most natural purpose.

Natural human systems don't work every time nor according to a watch on a nervous wrist. But living systems are the only things that work, especially over the cycles of time we call generations. In any given span even the most skillful and diligent leadership may fail. Bad people succeed in accumulating another pile of cruel dividends torn from the hopes of the poor. Again. But every greedy despot and over-clever thief has seen their end, the dilution of what they thought theirs. Still, in any one leader's life the time may run short, leaving their hopes unfulfilled.

Some of us recently met Larry James, a generative leader in a tough city divided between rich and poor. Despite decades of work on poverty and discrimination with an amazing team of people in a place they loved, not much had changed. That's tough to face but it only sharpened the edge of his clarity about measuring his life. We asked him about his hope, noting that Walter Rauschenbusch, hopeful voice of a great movement of mercy and justice in the early 1900s, died in despair when he saw the social justice movement captured by the war spirit of the day. Quietly, after what seemed a long time, Larry said, "I can see that." And after a pause: "But I'd rather die in despair than live as a hypocrite."

Larry's is not a blind hope, sustained only by ignoring the painful evidence of too few years against enduring patterns. Quite the opposite. His hope is not measured by one lifespan, the sum of his personal best efforts over five or six decades. Pity that kind of arithmetic. What he sees clearly is that his life—including its relentless commitment to do its work every day—inspires others who bring their best, too.

I'd rather die in despair than live as a hypocrite

None are adequate apart, but they are enough to carry on a fair fight for as long as life needs. The sum of all those sums adds up to a remarkable array of landmarks to that kind way of life. Larry would squirm at the comparison, but he basically answers the test of reality as did Jesus: "come, look, tell what you see; the hungry are fed, the prisoners visited, the homeless sheltered, the unemployable find honorable work."

As with Larry, the promise of generative leadership is that we can live our lives aligned with the great flow of life and its certain fruits of mercy, justice and kindness without being swept into happy talk or the ways of violence and death. We can choose life and we can actually tell the difference. At least, if we hang around those in urgent love, with the people and places for whom we hope. No generative leader survives a day without their company of generative agents. They can't even remember the point of their life apart from the movement that calls.

But together we can. We can do that. You can do that. With life it's as simple and certain as water finding its way down the river to the sea.

REFERENCES

CHAPTER 3

1. For their book on this, see Douglas R. McGaughey and James R. Cochrane, *The Human Spirit: Groundwork* (Stellenbosch, South Africa: SUN Press, 2017).
2. Stubbs, Aelred (ed.), *I Write What I Like: Steve Biko, A Selection of His Writings* (Oxford: Heinemann, 1987), p.87ff.

CHAPTER 4

1. See (https://oxfamilibrary.openrepository.com/bitstream/handle/10546/620599/bp-public-good-or-private-wealth-210119-summ-en.pdf?utm_source=indepth)
2. Susan Wilkinson-Maposa, Alan Fowler, Ceri Oliver-Evans and Chao F.N. Mulenga, "The Poor Philanthropist—How and why the poor help each other," 2009, University of Cape Town-Graduate School of Business: "A key message of this inquiry is that people who are poor know something about getting resources to where they are most needed. The intent is, therefore, to ensure that this local knowledge is recognised, listened to, learned from and properly considered in organised philanthropy and social investment support in Southern Africa." (p. xii).
3. Meas Nee, *Towards Restoring Life in Cambodian Villages* (JSRC Phnom Penh, 1999), Ch. 5, http://www.amazon.com/Towards-Restoring-Life-Cambodian-Villages/dp/B001O8WHUS
4. Fynbos (/feɪnbɒs/, Afrikaans pronunciation: [ˈfɛɪnbos], meaning 'fine-leaved plants') is a unique botanical vegetation found in the Western Cape and Eastern Cape provinces of South Africa, a small area known as the Cape Floral Kingdom, far the smallest of six such kingdoms in the world, with more diversity than anywhere else.
5. Personal email exchange, April 2019.

CHAPTER 5

1. EASUN (www.easuncentre.org), *Turning Points*, Newsletter, issue no. 9, December 2017, pp. 2-3.

CHAPTER 6

1. Adapted from Neil Gaiman, *Art Matters* (London: Headline Publishing, 2018).
2. Martin Dempsey and Ori Brafman, *Radical Inclusion: What the Post-9/11 World Should Have Taught Us About Leadership* (Missionday, 2018).

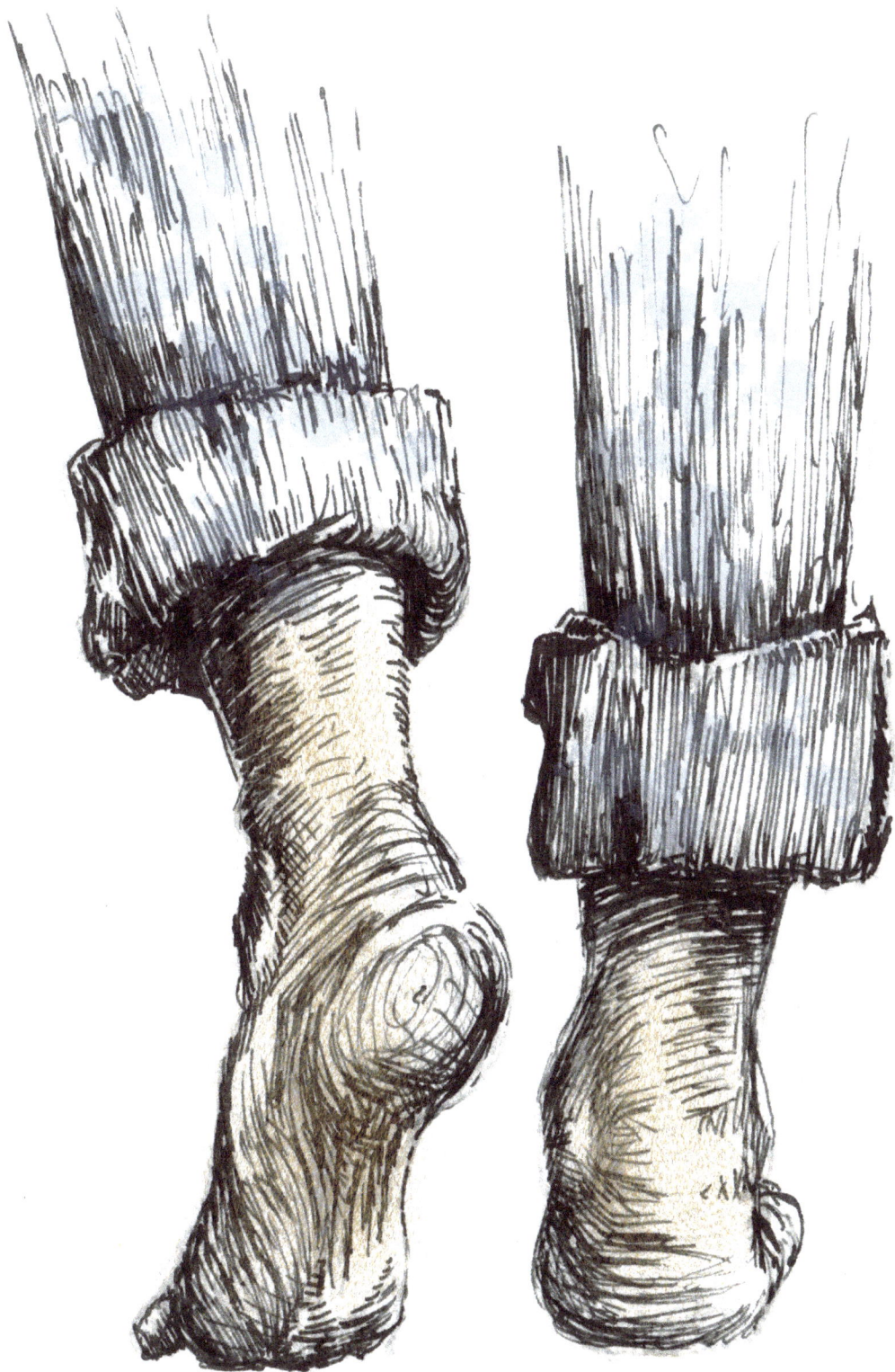

www.ingramcontent.com/pod-product-compliance
Lightning Source LLC
Chambersburg PA
CBHW060957030426
42334CB00032B/3272